HOME BUSINESS TAX SAVINGS

MADE EASY!

The MORE You KNOW,
the LESS You OWE!

5th Edition, Revised

RONALD R. MUELLER, MBA, Ph.D.

Published by Home Business Tax Savings, Inc.

Home Business Tax Savings, *MADE EASY!* ™
The MORE You KNOW, the LESS You OWE!™

It's How Much You *KEEP*, That Counts! Not how much you Make™
The ONLY Plain English Step-by-Step Guide to Home-Business Tax Breaks Authorized by Congress™

Cover Design
Michael Cartwright
macartwright@comcast.net

Layout & Design
Ginger Marks
DocUmeant Designs
www.DocUmeantDesigns.com

Library of Congress Control Number 2005900318

ISBN: 978-0-9707538-9-2
[10 Digit ISBN: 0-9707538-9-6]

CONTENTS

DEDICATIONS AND ACKNOWLEDGMENTS

I dedicate this book first and foremost to **GOD**, without Whom nothing is possible (John 15:15).

A special debt of thanks goes to my good friend and one of my personal mentors **ROBERT G. ALLEN**. One of his many #1 bestsellers, *Multiple Streams of Income* and its phenomenal success, stimulated me to write this book. Everyone who reads Bob's books and follows his advice, will have one or more home-businesses, and thus be able to reap massive benefits from <u>this</u> 'Plain English' tax-savings guide.

I also acknowledge my parents **Clare and Betty Mueller** who instilled in me the core values of integrity, honesty and a sense of humor – all of which I hope are evident throughout this book.

Finally I want to acknowledge my "inner circle."

> **Lisa Stevens** joined me fulltime in March 2008 after three years as executive assistant to one of my own mentors, Robert Allen. Lisa handles a myriad of customer service questions and special requests daily, makes sure all orders are shipped immediately, schedules all of my on-stage presentations and live webinars/teleseminars, and keeps thousands of details from 'falling through the cracks.'

Sandra Lynch handles customer care and devotes countless hours researching complex tax issues to ensure the absolute accuracy of the information you read in this book. Sandy also is my bookkeeper, my tax research guru, my colleague and my friend.

Albert Isensee, the seasoned expert in home business tax law who I turn to when I get stumped on a tax question (albert@taxman.bz).

FOREWORD BY ROBERT G. ALLEN

For more than two decades I have been writing, lecturing, teaching and coaching thousands of people about the importance of establishing multiple streams of income. I've been on the New York Times bestseller list with numerous books including *Nothing Down, Creating Wealth, Multiple Streams of Income, Multiple Streams of Internet Income, The One Minute Millionaire* and *Cash in a Flash.*

The media has referred to me as "the millionaire-maker" because of the great number of people who have taken my message to heart, acted on the advice I gave them, and became self-made millionaires.

Ron Mueller, the author of this amazing step-by-step guide, is one of my protégés and has been a close personal friend for several years. Ron's book delivers a truly important message:

No matter how *many* streams of income you put into place,

No matter how *large* those streams grow to become,

No matter how *successful* each stream turns out...

Ultimately, as the *original* title of this book said,
"It's How Much You *KEEP*, That Counts!
Not how much you Make."

This authoritative guide is thoroughly researched and carefully documented, **but it is also fun to read and easy to use** – no kidding!   In a word, it is *invaluable*.

With this information, anyone can understand and use all of the tax laws Congress has passed in order to encourage average Americans to establish and run small and home-based businesses.

I'm not aware of any other material like this available anywhere. Nothing this complete, this straight-forward, this fun to read, and this easy to use.

"Home Business Tax Savings *MADE EASY*" holds a valuable place in my own personal resource library. Congratulations to you for making it a part of yours too. But don't just put this on your bookshelf. Use it! My own businesses are all based in my own home, for the very reasons Ron describes in this terrific guide.

Do you want to know a secret? **A simple home-based business offers more tax breaks than the super-wealthy can get with their expensive tax lawyers.** That's no lie!

You know, I've always thought that reading about tax-law was about as exciting as watching paint dry. But in *this* book, Ron actually makes tax-law fun to read about! I promise, you will actually enjoy reading this material! This is a "light read" with a "powerful impact."

Everyone with a home-based business needs this book!

Anyone <u>without</u> a home-based business needs it <u>even more</u>!

Financial Freedom is an attainable goal. I think the most powerful way to accomplish it is to:

- Establish multiple streams of income,

- Focus on streams that produce residual income, and

- Use the tax laws wisely in order to ensure that you are paying only the minimum required by law.

My own books will help you with the first two, but THIS BOOK is what you will need for the last one.

Prosperously yours,

Robert G. Allen

"According to a new poll, seven out of ten Americans say our tax code is too complicated. Well, of course, it's complicated. That's why they call it a 'code.' They don't <u>want</u> you to understand."

Jay Leno, April 2005

WHY CAN YOU TRUST WHAT'S IN THIS BOOK?

By profession, the author is not a tax lawyer, a CPA, or an Enrolled Agent. That's why I am able to write in "plain English."

I am an investigative journalist. A journalist who asks good questions, who probes until I get answers that make sense, who follows up on every lead, who checks out every inconsistency, and who doesn't report *anything* until I thoroughly understand *everything* I can about the topic I'm writing about.

In 1999 decided I had enough of sucking-up exhaust fumes and following tail lights. I had heard all my life that when you work for yourself – even with a part time business – you get lots of new tax deductions. But nobody had ever told me exactly what those tax breaks are, or how to qualify for them or what records I would need to keep.

So I went to a book store; then to another book store, looking for a guide to tax breaks available to part-time home-based business owners. When I couldn't find what I was looking for, I went online. When that failed me also, I even went to the Library of Congress, which has a copy of every book ever copyrighted in America. Nothing.

Now, as an investigative reporter, I am wondering if these "big tax breaks" I had heard about, were real, or were just an urban legend.

By then my curiosity was piqued, and I set out on a personal mission to uncover the truth. I started by interviewing CPAs. **One of the first things I discovered absolutely shocked me!**

It's a fact – an understanding of home-based business tax law is not taught in most accounting schools, and isn't even tested on the CPA exam! Not one question! Even CPA Continuing Education in most states has nothing to offer on home-based business tax law.

Like millions of Americans, I used to turn to CPAs for tax advice every year, assuming they knew all of the legal tax deductions. I admit that I was naïve. I had no idea that of the monstrous size of the Tax Code.

> **"Standard Federal Tax Reporter" is some 44,656 pages published in 22 volumes, and it *grows by an average of 50 pages per week!***
>
> **The Bible contains approximately 800,000 words. The Tax Code contains approximately 9,000,000 words -- about as long as 11 Bibles!**
>
> **The IRS pays some 115,000 employees to interpret and enforce the bewildering array of tax laws.**

No one can be an expert in everything contained in a bookcase full of tax law! So simply finding a person with the initials CPA after his or her name, is no indication whether they do, or do not, know ANYTHING about home-based business tax law. In most cases, they will know it only if they are self-taught.

If I needed surgery, I would automatically seek out a specialist. I now know that I need to do the same for tax preparation. The right surgeon can save my life. The right tax advisor can save my financial life.

By interviewing enough tax preparers and tax advisors, I did find enough who were experts in this narrow area of tax law, to give direction to my investigation.

Since no one can possibly understand all of categories of all of the tax laws, tax preparers need to specialize, and the 33-million home-business owners in the U. S. need to work with one who specializes in home-business tax law.

Along the way I discovered that there really ARE tax breaks for business owners (yes, even for part time businesses), and they are NOT "loopholes" or "tax dodges" or "gray areas."

The Home-Business Tax Breaks Passed by Congress Were NOT an Accidental by-product of Clever Lawyers

Congress didn't create laws that ended up "unintentionally" decreasing Federal tax revenues because some clever lawyers found a loophole. No, they passed these laws for two specific and important reasons.

The **first objective** was to stimulate the strongest segment of the American economy – small business. But the **biggest objective** was to encourage every taxpayer to have a home-based business, and to continue to run it actively, because it provides the ideal "safety net" in times of economic downturns and layoffs.

If you find out tomorrow that you are unemployed, what would you do? You _could_ go home to look up the address of the unemployment office. But it would be far better for the economy if, instead, you went home to ramp-up your part-time home-based business to FULL-time.

That being Congress' objective, the question they wrestled with was, "How do we motivate busy people to do something else?" Answer? What's the greatest motivator of all time?

Right – money.

Money may not be the most important thing for a lot of people, but it does tend to rank up there with oxygen for a whole lot of folks! Do you think money is not important? If so, let me ask you a question – would you hit the snooze button, or would you get out of bed, for a job if you didn't get paid? I rest my case.

So Congress decided they'd PAY taxpayers to start and to run a home-based business. The method of payment – HUGE TAX REFUNDS.

Their next question was, "What should we require them to do to qualify for these huge tax breaks?"

Well, the objective was for taxpayers to have a part-time business <u>they could ramp-up to full-time if the need arose</u>, so the requirements were (and still are) simple:

1. **Have a Profit-Intent.**

   Note the word "intent." They wanted to incentivize us to *start* a home business so the tax breaks begin as soon as we begin <u>trying</u> to make a profit.

2. **Work your business on a Regular and Consistent basis.**

   Why this requirement? If we started a home-based business, but didn't keep working it on a regular basis, we would NOT have a part-time business *that we could ramp-up to full-time without notice.*

3. **'Run your Business like a Business,' keeping good records.**

   Treat your small, part-time business just like the big, full-time business you may want (or need) it to be.

That's it! If you meet those three requirements, you can qualify for a boatload of new, additional tax refunds.

Let there be no doubt, the government **wants** your tax money! But they want a stable economy even more.

Consider these Census Bureau statistics:

- **Small Businesses in the U. S., total approximately 22.9 million (and growing rapidly)**

- **Of those, 12.1 million (53%) are home-based**

- **Small businesses make up more than 99.7% of all employers**

- **Small businesses employ about 50% of all private sector workers**

- **Small businesses create 75% of new jobs in our national economy**

- **4 years after start-up, 50% of all small businesses <u>remain open</u>.**

That set of statistics paints an amazing picture, doesn't it?

The bottom line is this: Congress has passed a series of tax laws <u>for the intended purpose</u> of encouraging and rewarding average Americans who will operate small or home-based businesses. Why? Because <u>it's good for the national economy</u>.

My research took about 12 months, followed by a six month dedication to <u>translating it into English</u> – from legal-*ese*, IRS-*ese* , and government-*ese*. The result is this easy to read, easy to use, step-by-step guide you now have in your hands.

I strongly believe we should each willingly pay Uncle Sam every penny required by law. But the law does *not* require any of us to *over*-pay!

When you learn about some deductions in this Guide that intrigue you, and then you go ask your own tax preparer about them, he or she just may say, "I don't think that's allowed."

Why? **BECAUSE THEY DON'T KNOW!**

Why don't they know? As stated earlier, they have never learned the narrow, **but crucial**, area of taxes called "home-business tax law."

But you shouldn't have to fight with your tax preparer about the legality of these deductions, so here's what you will find throughout this guide:

Following every major deduction we describe in this guide, you will find, right here in black and white, the <u>exact</u> **Congressional Law**, the <u>specific</u> Article in the **U.S. Tax Code**, or the <u>precise</u> Federal Tax Court Ruling which specifically <u>authorizes it.</u>

So, when your tax advisor says that one of these deductions is not legal, point them to the source cited right here in this book. When he or she consults the sources we cite for you, they can arrive at only one conclusion – **the deductions described here are 100% legal, ethical, safe, proper and honest.**

The IRS reviewed this book, and when they finished, they didn't ask for a single change!

It's not your tax pro's "fault" they don't know about them. They never had an opportunity <u>or incentive</u> to learn home-business tax law – *until now*.

After discovering *HUGE* tax deductions <u>you</u> have missed out on, due to <u>their</u> lack of knowledge, you may consider giving them a copy of this book and saying to them:

> *"I intend to take advantage of far more deductions than you've ever told me about before, and I can <u>prove</u> that each one is 100% IRS-compliant. I need for you to learn this stuff, or I will have to begin working with another tax advisor."*

Then do what you need to.

LET'S GET INTO IT

Everybody thinks they are paying too much in taxes, yet it is a rare person who does anything about it.

Congratulations! By actively running a small or home-based business with the intent to make a profit, you have created a second stream of income *and* begun to *qualify* for the <u>huge</u> tax breaks described in this guide. By reviewing this information, you put yourself into that small percentage of the population willing to at least **consider** taking some actions to reduce your taxes to the minimum required by law.

The working American's average wage today is about $28,000. That works out to $13.50/hour. Not much, huh? But that's *before taxes*! <u>After</u> taxes, the average American worker only takes home about **$8.00 an hour!**

Let me ask you a question: If someone offered to show you a legal way to significantly reduce your **mortgage** or **rent** payments, or to slash the size of your **car** payment, would you be interested? Of course!

Why, then, do most people freeze in their tracks when offered information on how to reduce their **taxes**?

The three main reasons:

> (1) Fear of the IRS,

> (2) Fear of the time it will take to keep detailed records, and

> (3) Not fully understanding what deductions are legal.

Here's good news for you on all three counts!
No Need to Fear the IRS

If you're *not* a shoplifter, do you care one way or the other about those theft detectors at the exit door of the drug store? Why would you? Or if you're driving and have not been drinking, do you fear being stopped by police at a breathalyzer checkpoint? No, because you have nothing to fear if you haven't been drinking.

When you obey the law, there is no reason to fear law enforcement.

Well, if you understand and follow tax laws passed by Congress and authorized in the Internal Revenue Code, would you have any reason to fear a tax audit?

Look, if you have three dependents, do you "play it safe" on your Tax Returns by claiming only two of them? No way! Why not? Because you know what the tax law allows and you know how to count to three. It's that simple.

Well then, you will not need to "play it safe" by not claiming the legal tax deductions passed by Congress to benefit your business – once you understand the tax laws.

A taxpayer's chance of being audited is only about one percent, but even if you *are* audited, you'll have <u>nothing to fear</u> once you understand the laws and are staying within them.

For people who carefully follow this guide and get tax advice from experts in home-business tax law, an audit would simply be an "unavoidable inconvenience" – not something to be feared.

Documentation –
It's Not as Bad as You Think!

This guide will show you how spending a minute or so a day keeping records, could qualify you for substantial tax deductions every year – resulting in up to $5,000 or more in tax refunds for many (possibly *most*) taxpayers.

There IS Another way to put an
extra $5,000 in your pocket…

You could take-on another part-time job. But you would have to make $13.50/hour and work *at least* 12 hours a week, 50 weeks a year, to put $5,000 after-tax cash into your pocket.

OR, Option Two, you could spend one hour a day, three or four days a week running a home-based business you enjoy instead of working 12 hours every week for a full year at a part time job you'd most likely hate… and seeing your family even less than now.

Financially, the result is the same either way. Which would you rather do?

As you read this guide, you're going to discover that it is amazingly easy to qualify for thousands and thousands of dollars in legal tax deductions that you had no idea about before.

Oh, by the way, this book is NOT about

- **Loopholes**

- **Tax-Dodges**

- **Gray-Areas**

- **Tax Evasion Schemes, or**

- **IRS-Bashing.**

As said earlier, every tax deduction described in this step-by-step guide is based on an Act of Congress, a Section in the Tax Code, or a Tax Court Ruling. Think about it – since the laws themselves allow so many **100%** **legal** deductions for home-business operators, who needs to take on the risky ones? Not you, and *definitely not me!*

A minute ago we discussed why you should have no fear of the IRS. **First**, the chance of an audit is only about two percent – that's only 2 out of every

100 people. And **second**, even if you end up being one of the 2 out of the 100, it'll be an easy audit, since the **specific reference** which authorizes every single deduction you claim, is right here in this book.

With a tax return prepared in compliance with the law and properly documented, the IRS Auditor will likely stamp your return:

ACCEPTED AS FILED

Why? Most likely you were selected at random by an IRS computer program, and the purpose of most audits of an individual, a sole proprietor or an LLC, is simply to see if a taxpayer qualified for all the deductions he or she claimed. By following the advice in "Home Business Tax Savings, *Made Easy!"* you will be able to establish that very quickly with an Auditor.

The Auditor's job is to reach into your pocket and extract cash, but they can only do that if you are trying to cheat on your taxes or have filed inaccurate returns or claimed undocumented deductions.

Why would an Auditor want to waste his or her time going over the Tax Return of a taxpayer who can very quickly establish that he/she understands the tax laws, has followed them carefully, and has kept the required records? They will say, "Thank you for your time," and go drop their fishhook in a different pond.

Thoughts on 'Legitimate Tax Avoidance'
by former Unites States Supreme Court
Justice Louis D. Brandeis

"I live in Alexandria, Virginia. Near the Supreme Court chambers is a toll bridge across the Potomac River. When in a rush, I pay the one-dollar toll and get home early. However, I usually drive a mile outside the downtown section of the city, and cross the Potomac on the free bridge.

This bridge was placed outside of downtown Washington, D.C. to serve a useful social service: getting drivers to drive the extra mile to help alleviate congestion during the rush hour.

If I drive over the toll bridge and through the toll-barrier without paying the toll, I would be committing tax evasion.

If, however, I drive the extra mile outside the city of Washington, I am using a legitimate, logical and suitable method of tax avoidance, and I am performing a useful social service by doing so.

For tax evasion, I should be punished. For tax avoidance, I should be commended.

The tragedy of life today is that so few people know that the free bridge even exists."

This book is your map to the 'free bridges.

CHAPTER ONE

The United States Has TWO Tax Systems
(And YOU Just Might be in the WRONG ONE!)

The United States has one tax system for **employees**, which includes most working Americans, and a very different – and much better – tax system for **business owners**.

Employees are very limited in what they can write-off, but **Business Owners** engaged in earning (or working *toward* earning) profits, are entitled to a wide variety of legally deductible business expenses in their pursuit of that income and profit.

In this Guide, you will learn how YOU can legally and easily qualify for nearly all of the same tax breaks big businesses get year after year, even with just a part-time home-based business.

First, a little background on America's tax system… Or, we should use the plural, tax system<u>s</u>, since we have just said there are two tax systems in America.

The first type of Taxpayer is the
Employee

Employees, or W-2 wage earners, work for someone else. Most taxpayers fall into this category. They have very few tax deductions available to them, usually just

- Mortgage interest & Real Estate taxes,

- Standard deductions for dependents,

- Gifts to church or charity and

- Contributions to a retirement plan.

Essentially, for employees, it's a three-step process:

Step 1: Work hard to earn a decent wage.

Step 2: Immediately lose a huge chunk of those hard-earned wages to taxes.

Step 3: Then you get to live on the leftovers, called take-home-pay.

The Second Type of Taxpayer is the
Business Owner

Business Owners, on the other hand, get to write-off lots and lots of expenses, from rent to phone bills to furniture to cleaning crews.

Business Owners have a **very different** three-step tax system:

Step 1: Earn revenue from selling goods or services,

Step 2: Spend whatever they need to on operating expenses to keep the business financially solid,

Step 3: **Then** pay taxes **only** on whatever is **left over**.

The long list of deductions commonly available to **Business Owners**, include:

- Mortgage interest or Rent
- **Gas, electric, water and sewer**
- Cleaning crews to dust, vacuum and empty the trash
- **Computers, copiers, fax machines and telephones**
- Advertising
- **Paper, pens and postage**
- Bank fees on business accounts
- **Desks, sofas, coffee tables and other furniture**
- Credit card annual fees (for business-only cards)
- **Depreciation**
- Painting, wallpaper, carpeting and other repairs/maintenance

- **Legal and professional services**
- Bad debts from sales or services (accrual method)
- **Phones bills, cell-phones, pagers and Personal Digital Assistants**
- Cost of goods sold
- **Magazines and books for business education**
- Newspapers, magazines, books and on-line media
- **Services performed by Independent Contractors**
- Supplies and materials
- **Plane fares, hotel costs, meals and rental cars**
- Taxes and licenses
- **Special work clothing or uniforms**
- Lunches, dinners, ball games and theater tickets
- **Security alarms and hidden cameras**
- Health, life, dental, vision, disability and unemployment insurance
- **Company cars (and even boats)**
- Contributions to Employee Retirement Plans
- **Holiday cards, gifts and postage.**
- And any other expense that qualifies as "ordinary and necessary" to operate their business.

If you operate an **Internet *eCommerce* Business**, your deductions might **also** include:

- **Internet access fees**
- Merchant discount fees
- **Web hosting fees**
- Cable, DSL or Broadband internet service
- **Computer extended-warranty costs**

- Database backup services
- **Ink and Toner cartridges for printers**
- Software used for business
- **Spyware and Antivirus subscription services**
- Firewalls
- **Routers**
- Peripherals
- **Surge-protection equipment**
- Conference call services

If you operate an **Insurance** or **Real Estate Business**, your deductions might **also** include:

- **Advertising**
- Commissions
- **Licenses**
- Professional fees
- **Sponsorships**
- Chamber of Commerce membership
- **Signs and promotional materials**
- Continuing education courses
- **Insurance**
- Seminars & Conferences
- **Permits & fees**
- Cell phone, pager and voicemail
- **Printing, copying and faxing**
- and much more.

If You are an *Employee*, How Much are You *Really* Paying in Taxes?

The answer may astound you! Taxes represent **_by far_** the LARGEST single bill the average American employee pays! The amount withheld from your paycheck for taxes <u>before you even see it</u> is probably more than your mortgage or rent, *PLUS* your car payment, *PLUS* your food costs, and *PLUS* health care expenses -- **COMBINED**!

When you add together Federal taxes, State taxes, Social Security taxes, Medicare taxes, sometimes County or City taxes, and all the rest, if you're like the "average" wage earner in America, **you could easily be losing HALF of your hard earned wages to taxes, <u>before</u> you even <u>see</u> your paycheck**!

Now, most people believe in paying their "fair share" of taxes, but do you think **_half_** <u>of your hard-earned wages</u> is "your fair share?"

Do You Know WHY our Government uses "Payroll Deduction" as its Method of Collecting Income Taxes?

Here's an educated guess ...

What if you earned $1,000 in wages, and your employer put it all in your paycheck, but **_then_** as soon as you got it, you **_immediately_** had to <u>write a check to the government</u> for $400 for your taxes (40%), leaving you only

$600 out of your hard-earned $1,000 to live on? What do you think would happen?

There would be a taxpayer revolt that would make the Boston Tea Party look like child's play, that's what would happen!

So what does our government do? They make your employer withhold all those taxes from your wages _**first**_, and then just give you the part that is _**left over**_ after taxes have been siphoned out.

That way, they're hoping you won't realize how much of a huge bite Uncle Sam is taking out of your pay!

The **IRS collected $2 TRILLION** from nearly 200 million taxpayers last year. And "Enforcement Actions" (their term for Audits) raked in **another $50 Billion**. Those numbers are from the IRS Commissioner himself!

The only way to snatch $2 Trillion out the pockets of 200 Million American workers without a revolt is to <u>withhold it before you see it</u>, showing you only the part left-over – commonly referred to as take-home pay.

Now, IMAGINE for a Moment …

How much less would you pay in taxes if you only had to pay Uncle Sam a percentage of **your after-expenses "leftover money,"** like businesses do, instead of paying a percentage of the gross wages you earn, like you do now? You would pay a whole lot less in taxes, that's for sure!

What if you were allowed legally to treat a portion of your home like an "office-building space" (which is tax-deductible), and what if you could convert some of the expenses you're already paying for, into "business expenses" (which are also tax-deductible)? Do you think that would make a difference in the taxes you pay?

Yes, a major difference!

Here's the Good News You Have Been Waiting For…

It **is** possible for an **individual** to get most of the **same tax breaks** as a "big" business owner can get -- and even more!

But before we continue, I have to ask you an important question …

Would you mind if it turned out to be <u>both</u> 100% legal <u>and</u> really **EASY to cut your taxes significantly?** Would it be okay if what I'm about to share with you is not at all complicated?

I'm serious. Some people really believe, "No pain, no gain." And many believe that if it has to do with taxes, "if it's easy and legal, my tax guy would have told me about it." <u>Don't believe either one</u>! They're both wrong, as you are discovering for yourself.

But first, let me share with you a story that I'm told is true.

Back when Coca Cola was a new company, their business was selling syrup to "soda fountains," which then combined it with carbonated water to make a soft drink called a "Coke."

One day a visitor called on the Chairman of the Coca Cola Company in Atlanta, and said to him:

"If you decide to act on the idea I am about to share with you, will you give me one-half of one percent of the profits you make from it?"

The Chairman agreed, of course, because if the idea was a good one, he'd gladly pay ½ of 1%, because the Coca Cola Company would still get to keep 99½%. And if the idea wasn't any good, it wouldn't cost him anything. So the visitor leaned over and whispered these two words:

"Bottle it."

Those two words very quickly made the visitor a multi-millionaire.

Was the idea complicated? **Of course not.**

Was the idea powerful? **<u>Absolutely!</u>**

Why did I want to share that little story with you? Because, just like "Bottle it," what I am about to share with you is **not complicated**, <u>and</u> is **very, very powerful!**

If you operate a legitimate *home*-based business with the intent to produce a profit, you can qualify for most of the same deductions as an "*office*-based" business.

In addition, even *more* expenses associated with your home office become deductible as your business turns profitable.

If you're wondering when this amazing new set of tax laws were passed and why you haven't heard about them, this is going to surprise you: **Almost *nothing* in this guide is new.** Seriously!

Most of these Tax Laws, Tax Codes and Tax Court Rulings have been in place for three or more years, and even the newest ones were made retroactive. So most of them are not new -- just new to <u>you</u>.

VERY IMPORTANT ADVICE:

No one should ever start a home-based business for the purpose of getting new tax deductions. That's not the intent of the law and frankly it just doesn't work. Tax deductions should be the *result* of having a home-based business, *not* the *reason* for it.

[IRC Section 280A(c)]

Are you just starting up your own business? If so, here is MORE Great News!

This tax benefit is relatively new. Congressional law now allows taxpayers to elect to deduct up to $5,000 in new-business Start-Up Costs *AND* $5,000 in Organizational Expenditures <u>in the tax year in which their business begins</u>. This is a huge *new* benefit for small and home-based businesses.

Start up costs are those expenses which you incur before you actually begin offering goods or services for sale. Organizational costs are expenses for business license or setting up a business entity such as an LLC or Corporation.

By the time you finish reading this book, you will have a thorough understanding of three things that the vast majority of American taxpayers (and most tax *preparers*) do not understand in the least:

- Exactly <u>what</u> deductions the tax laws <u>allow</u>,
- How to <u>qualify</u> to use them to reduce <u>your own</u> taxes to the legal minimum, and
- What <u>records</u> will make your Tax Returns "Bullet Proof."

The legal right of a taxpayer to decrease the amount of what otherwise would be his taxes, or altogether avoid them by means which the law permits, cannot be doubted."

Unites States Supreme Court
in case of
Gregory v. Helvering, 293 US 465

CHAPTER TWO

Your Home-Based Business Could Legally Qualify You for Thousands of Dollars in New Tax Breaks!

This is the equivalent to "Bottle it," as we discussed in Chapter One. It's **uncomplicated** like "Bottle it." <u>And</u> it is just as **powerful** as "Bottle it!"

Many people who don't have a home-based business aren't even looking for one. Why? Because they're too busy at their job (or jobs) trying to earn enough after-tax money to make ends meet. Do you have a "traditional" W-2 job? You know what the word JOB stands for, don't you? My friend Robert Allen, who wrote the Foreword to this book, says a **J.O.B.** stands for **Just Over Broke!**

First we chuckle at that, but then we realize it's TRUE! In fact, for many of us, the word should be spelled **JUB** for Just <u>Under</u> Broke since most of the time we run out of money before we run out of month.

That's why the average American household today holds 2.5 jobs and is $7,000 *or more* in credit card debt! Isn't that sad?

But it doesn't have to be this way!

You are already learning several things you probably didn't know before, and you are about to discover that several things you <u>thought</u> you knew about home businesses and the tax law, just are <u>not correct</u>.

Myth #1:

"My tax guy told me that I have to show a profit in three out of every five years, or else I'll lose all my tax-deductions."

The Truth:

That's pure garbage. To qualify as a bona fide business, you only have to prove your **intent** to produce a **profit** and to work the business **actively** and **regularly**. You could potentially claim losses year after year (with no specified limit) as long as you can **prove** that you have the **intent** to produce a profit and are actively working toward that goal. Where does this "3 out of 5" thing come from? It comes from an internal IRS document called, "Audit Procedures Guide," that says, *"If a taxpayer's business has been profitable in any 3 of the past 5 years, they are <u>presumed</u> to have a profit-intent."* But then it <u>goes on to say</u>, *"If they have <u>not</u> been profitable in 3 of the past 5* *years, there is **no presumption** that that activity was not engaged in for profit... Examiners cannot rely on lack of profit alone as the basis for disallowing losses."*

[Reg Sec 1.183-2(a) and (d)]

> **NOTE: In just a few pages, we will show you exactly how to prove your "profit intent." A simple Business Plan is one key to satisfying the requirements. You can download a fill in the blanks draft of a Business Plan to adapt to your own business, by going online to www.HomeBusinessTaxSavings.com.**

Unless you've been living under a rock you've heard of Amazon.com. They legally wrote off millions in business losses for many years in a row. How was that legal?   Because they could **prove** they had an **intent** to produce a profit, <u>and you can too</u>!

Myth #2:

"I can only write-off a room and the equipment and furniture in it if I use it <u>exclusively</u> for my business."

The Truth:

That's the "Exclusive Use Rule," which does apply to home-office deductions, **but** you do **not** have to use an **entire room** exclusively. You can use a "visually identifiable space" -- meaning a portion of a room that "looks like an office," although that area must be used exclusively for business. Even if you have a one room apartment, you can put a table in one corner, put a computer, printer, and phone on the table, and pull a chair up to it – – and guess what? That's a "visually identifiable space."

Also, you'll soon learn when and how you could *also* write off some of the costs of furniture and equipment used wholly *or partially* for business whether they are in the exclusive use room(s) or not.

[IRC Section § 280 A(c)(2)]

Myth #3:

"I've been told that the amount of my write-offs can't be any greater than the amount of money I make in my home-business. If I just started my home-based business, why bother with all of this for now?"

The Truth:

What you've been told is a "partial truth." **Nearly all** home-business tax deductions can be applied against *any* source of income -- home-business, W-2 job, investment income, rental properties, retirement pay, etc. There are only two exceptions, and one of those two can be "banked" for use in any future year when your business does show a profit. *More on this later.*

"Intent to Produce a Profit."
What does that <u>Mean</u>, and How can I <u>Prove</u> it?

One of the three requirements for qualifying for home-business tax deductions, is to have a "profit intent." That means, simply, that you are <u>trying</u> to make a profit – i.e., that you are in business for the purpose of making a profit, *not* for the purpose of producing tax write-offs. (The first is honest, the second just doesn't work.)

Fortunately, some of the same activities that help you to build your business are those which the IRS looks for in proving your intent to make a profit. In other words, the specific actions you are taking to create profitability are the same actions that help to substantiate your deductions.

IRS Auditors use several "relevant factors" to determine whether or not your business qualifies for small/home business tax deductions.

[Reg. Sec. 1.183(b)]

Here are the main ones:

1. Does the <u>time and effort</u> put into the activity indicate an intention to make a profit?

> Work your business on a *regular* and *consistent* basis. The Federal Tax Court recently ruled in favor of a taxpayer who "worked her business 45 minutes a day, 4 to 5 days a week." The court said she

met the "regularly and consistently" test. You might use that as a guideline, although, in your case, you might decide to work your business 30 minutes a day, six days a week; or an hour a day four days a week. Regularity and consistency are more important than total of time spent on the business.

2. Does the taxpayer <u>depend on income</u> from the activity?

If you need income from this activity to survive financially, most likely you have a profit intent.

3. If there are <u>losses,</u> (a) are they due to circumstances beyond the taxpayer's control or (b) did they occur during the start-up phase of the business?

Losses are not a disqualifying factor, as long as there is a good reason for it.

4. Has the taxpayer changed methods of operation to <u>improve profitability</u>?

If your business has a string of unprofitable years, be able to show that you are taking some actions to change the pattern, and turn profitable. If you run the same business (the "Activity") year after year, and it loses money year after year, and the amount of your losses is *not decreasing*, change something about how you are running your

business, change businesses, hire a business success coach – do
something!

5. Does the taxpayer or <u>his/her advisors</u> have the knowledge needed to carry on the activity as a successful business?

You, personally, do not have to be an expert, even in your own business category, IF you are actively learning from someone who IS an expert. If your company provides "trainings," including ones conducted by conference calls, and you participate in them regularly, your conference notes and notations in your day planner will document your "effort to establish expertise."

6. Has the taxpayer <u>made a profit</u> in similar activities <u>in the past</u>?

If your business has a string of unprofitable years, but you can show that you have been profitable in a similar business in the past, they'll probably cut you more slack because you can show you have the ability to make money.

7. Does the activity make a <u>profit in some years</u>?

Some years, marketplace conditions may keep you from making a profit, so if you have been profitable in some years, and not profitable in other years, that is not a negative towards qualifying as a "legitimate business."

8. Can the taxpayer expect to make a _profit in the future_ from the _appreciation of assets_ used in the activity?

If your business is raising breeding horse, you will probably be unprofitable until your young horses (assets) are old enough to breed.

By the way, if your business has made a profit in any three of the past five years, you are <u>presumed</u> to carrying on your activity with a profit intent, in which case the above "factors" are not even considered.

All five Relevant Factors require good recordkeeping. This chore can be reduced to a minute or two a day by using either the $ixty $econd Tax $avings Organizer™ software program or the Tax MiniMi$er™ recordkeeping system. You'll find them both under "Products & Services" at www.HomeBusinessTaxSavings.com

---

CHAPTER THREE

Some of Your *Personal Expenses* Can Be Converted Into Valuable *Business Deductions*

A business is a business no matter what its size, whether or not it currently makes a profit, or where it is located.

This means as the owner of a small, part-time business run out of your home you should be treated no differently, for tax purposes, than the owner of a large business that is run out of a huge office building.

With a home-based business, your home is your office building, so the costs to maintain the business portion become tax-deductible expenses.

In order to really "get it," try this shift in thinking… Most people think of their street address as, "This is where I live, and also run a business here." Try, instead, thinking, "This is my place of business, where I also sleep."

Do that and you will intuitively understand many of the tax breaks for which your business can qualify.

What exactly <u>are</u> the "currently *non-deductible personal expenses*" you could convert into *tax-deductible* business expenses?

Here's a *partial* list of some of the tax-deductible expenses that businesses legally and routinely write-off, and some of the home-based business expenses that YOU can legally write-off, too.

NOTE:

Expenses referred to in this chapter may be deductible only if they are
- (1) **ordinary**,
- (2) **necessary**,
- (3) **reasonable** in amount, **and**
- (4) "**inextricably linked** to the production of income."

[IRC Section 280 A]

Legal **BUSINESS** Deductions	Legal **HOME-Business** Deductions
√ Mortgage Interest or Rent	√
√ **Gas, Electric, Water and Sewer**	√
√ Cleaning Service to Dust, Vacuum and Empty Trash	√
√ **Computers, Copiers, Fax Machines and Telephones**	√
√ Paper, Pens, Ink Cartridges and Postage	√
√ **Desks, Sofas, Coffee Tables and other Furniture**	√
√ Painting, Wallpaper, and other Repairs/Remodeling	√
√ **Phones Bills, Cell-Phones, Pagers and PDA's**	√

√	Newspapers, Magazines, Books and On-line Media	√
√	**Travel, Hotels, Meals, Rental Cars while Traveling**	√
√	Dinners, Ball Games and Theater Entertainment	√
√	**Security Alarms and Hidden Cameras**	√
√	Health, Dental, Disability and other Insurance	√
√	**Company Cars and even Boats**	√
√	Contributions to Employee Retirement Plans	√
√	**Pest Control and General Maintenance**	√
√	Holiday Cards and Postage and Gifts	√

It sure looks like the two columns of deductions are identical!

Of course **they're identical!** Remember that your street address is your place of business, and "business expenses are business expenses," whether the business is "housed" in a high-rise office building or "housed" in a suburban home or in-town apartment.

The primary difference is that, since your home is used for **both** business **and** personal purposes, you will need to define and provide support for the "deductible business portion" of your home-related expenditures. With the exception of your mortgage interest and property taxes, the business portion of the costs associated with maintaining your home (rent, insurance, maintenance, utilities, etc.) will be accumulated from year to year, so that you can use them as soon as your business becomes profitable.

Now let's look more closely at that list and see what it means in terms of Your Tax Savings...

Mortgage Interest **or Rent**

Yes, <u>Rent</u>! Finally, renters get a tax-break. Since business owners do not normally own the office building in which they have offices, why should you have to own the house in which your home-based business is based? You shouldn't, and the government agrees. Renters may now claim a business rent deduction on their Schedule C according to the Business Use Percentage (BUP) of their home. (The next section of this chapter shows you how to determine your BUP.)

Gas, Electric, Water and Sewer

Of course this not only includes the utilities themselves, but any equipment, repairs, service or maintenance. For example, installing new heat pump or furnace, adding a humidifier, buying salt for your water conditioner, repairing plumbing, replacing a well-pump, inspecting your furnace, cleaning your chimney and air ducts, etc. See Chapter Four for specifics on how much of these costs you can deduct.

Please NOTE:

"Double Deductions" may be available for some homeowners. Any taxpayer can claim Standard Deductions on their Form 1040 or they may itemize their deductions on a Schedule A (Itemized Deductions). But, as a home-based business owner, you may now be moving many of your personal Schedule A deductions over to Schedule C (Profit or Loss from Business). This may reduce your Schedule A "write-offs" to almost nothing. If that is the case with you, consider not filing a Schedule A at all, and take advantage of the "Standard Deduction" option on your Form 1040. worth $5.450 in 2009.

[IRS Publication 587]

Janitorial Service to Clean your Office Space

If you have a "maid service," you may qualify to deduct a portion of the fee you pay them. Or perhaps you can hire your kids (tax-deductible to you, tax-free to them – see Chapter Six) to perform those business services for you as "employees," instead of paying them a non-tax-deductible "allowance," which you'd pay out of your after-tax wages. In order to be deductible, their services must meet some requirements, which you'll learn about in Chapter Six.

Computers, Copiers, Fax Machines and Phones

Contrary to popular opinion, these items do NOT have to be used *exclusively* for business purposes, in order for you to be able to benefit from tax deductions. The next chapter shows you how to determine how much of the cost you can deduct. **[IRC Section § 280 F(d)(4) and IRS Publication 956]**

> **SPECIAL NOTE:** If you would like details and examples about depreciation and potential tax write-offs regarding business furniture and equipment, as well as laws about converting currently owned furniture and equipment from personal use to business use, consult with a tax professional who specializes in home business tax law.

Paper, Pens and Postage

Of course these items, and all other kinds of office supplies that are used for business purposes, are deductible for any business, including your own home-based business.

Desks, Sofas, Coffee Tables and other Furniture

The rule of thumb is "if you use it in your business, even only part time, at least a portion of the cost is probably deductible." Think about a traditional business run out of an office building. Don't you think they are 'tax-deducting' the cost of the sofa and coffee table in the lobby, the small round meeting tables and chairs in private offices, and even the coffee maker and water cooler in the kitchen? Of course, and you may be able to also. See Chapter Five for specifics on how much you can deduct.

Painting, Wallpaper, Carpeting and Maintenance

Many people think that "upgrades" may be deductible but "routine maintenance" is not. If you have a home-based business, that's not correct. That is the tax rule regarding deductibility of expenses associated with selling a home, but it has nothing to do with home-business deductions. As long as a portion of the home or apartment is used exclusively for business purposes, then at least part of maintenance expenses are probably deductible. See next chapter for specifics on how much you can deduct.

[IRS Publication 587]

Phone bills, Cell-phones, Pagers and PDAs

They're all deductible if they're used in your business, but there is one exception, and we'll cover that in detail in the next chapter.

[IRS Publication 587]

Newspapers, Magazines, Books and Online Media

Again, if you need it for your business, it's probably deductible. You probably don't need Reader's Digest for your business, but you may need Entrepreneur, or even a daily newspaper if you check the Classifieds for competitive intelligence and read the news pages for current news about your product category or about your customers.

Plane fares, Hotel costs, Meals, Rental cars

Expenses related to business travel are usually deductible, so if you can combine your personal travel with your business travel - and meet specific IRS rules - even personal travel (including "vacations") could become deductible.

[IRC Section 162(a)(2)]

Lunches, Ball Games and Theater Tickets

This is a category that confuses many people, but it's worth understanding because thousands of dollars worth of deductions are available under the right circumstances -- and those circumstances often are under your control. Much of the cost of "fun" could become legal business deductions.

Health, Dental and other types of Insurance

Under the right circumstances (consult your tax professional for ideal structuring), you can deduct not only the cost of the premiums, but also the annual deductibles, co-pays, etc.

Security Alarms, Motion Detectors and Hidden Cameras

A business owner needs to protect his or her place of business, and this is a normal cost of doing business (i.e., a legal tax deduction). By the way, when you think "alarm system," think broadly. If you install floodlights with motion detectors at your home (which is your place of business), you may be installing a security alarm system, which could be deductible.

[IRS Publication 587]

Company Cars and Even Boats

A car (or boat) does not have to be used exclusively for business purposes in order to be partially deductible. Chapter Eight will blow your mind, because the proper use of these rules could result in very large tax deductions for many businesses.

Contributions to Employee Retirement Plans

The rules are similar, whether you are an employee or a home-business owner, so be sure to take the deduction if it applies.

General Maintenance and Repairs

If you owned an office building, general maintenance costs would be deductible, right? The amount you can deduct for your home-business depends upon your "Business Use Percentage" (see next chapter).

[IRS Publication 587]

Holiday Cards, Postage and Gifts

They could be deductible, as long as they are "from your business" (i.e., not you, personally) and are for the primary purpose of promoting your business.

How about Health Insurance Premiums?

This recent change in the tax law can be worth a lot of money, as insurance premiums continue to soar out of sight.

If you are self-employed and are not included in any health insurance plan paid for (even partially) by an employer, you may be eligible to deduct 100% of your own health insurance premiums -- but only up to the amount of the net income (that means 'profit') from your business.

NOTE: This deduction applies **only** to sole proprietorships, single-owner LLCs, and C-Corporations, and is *not* subject to the 7.5% threshold that applies to other medical-related expenses.

In the parable of the talents in the New Testament, when the master learned that one servant had not been a good steward of the master's money, he "threw that worthless servant outside, into the darkness, where there will be weeping and gnashing of teeth."

Matthew 25: 14-30

Author's Note:

We are legally, ethically and honorably bound to pay every penny of taxes required under the law. But are we being good stewards of God's money if we <u>overpay</u> our taxes, instead of using that money for a much greater good? This book will show you how to reduce your taxes to the legal minimum.

CHAPTER FOUR

Determining Your Business Deductions when Your Business is Based in your Home

Remember all those non-deductible "personal" expenses we just discussed reclassifying as tax-deductible business expenses? Well, we cannot write-off 100% of those expenses, because after all, we do live there too. But we CAN write-off SOME of them.

What dollar amount or percentage of those expenses can you deduct? There are three categories of expenses and different (but easy) methods for calculating each. The only three terms you'll need to understand are:

> **1. Indirect Expenses**
>
> **2. Direct Expenses**
>
> **3. Business Assets**

INDIRECT Expenses:

Indirect Expenses are *indirectly* related to your home-business. Rent, utilities and general maintenance (such as replacing a roof or repainting the exterior of a house), are examples of ***Indirect Expenses***, because they are indirectly related to your business – i.e., you would have the same expenses whether you did or did not have a business based in the home. The amount of Indirect Expenses you can deduct depends upon the "Business Use Percentage" (BUP) of your home, and upon the profit of your home-based business.

What's the "BU" and what's the "P" in BUP?

First of all, the **"BU"** (business use) means an area of your home that is used regularly AND ***<u>EXCLUSIVELY</u>*** for business. Exclusively means just that – the area is <u>never</u> used for <u>anything</u> but business. The IRS has no sense of humor about this. If you ever admit that the area was used <u>even once</u> for your kids to do their homework – you lose the entire Home Office deduction.

Now about the **"P"** in BUP -- a Percentage of ***<u>what</u>***?

The Tax Code states, **"The taxpayer may use *any reasonable method* of determining the Business Use Percentage of his or her home."**

In the past most people have used the *finished* square footage of their home (i.e., it includes everything except your garage, barn, land, or unfinished basement or attic), but there is a newer option, which we will discuss in just a few minutes, that might be far more advantageous.

This tax deduction category begins, usually, with your **Home Office**, but it can include many additional areas of the home as well. The Tax Code **used to** require that a home office "have at least three walls around it." That pretty much requires use of a Separate Room, right? **But that changed last year**. The Code now says it simply must be a "visually identifiable space." What's that mean in English? It has to look like an office area. You know, table, chair, computer, etc. arranged in a way that it looks somewhat separated from the rest of the room it is in.

Now that we know what a home-office IS, what does it take to *qualify* to claim one on your tax return? It is now much easier to qualify, since Congress passed new legislation to "overrule" a Supreme Court decision.

To qualify for a home office, you now need only to pass any ONE of three tests. Your home-office must be

> Where the **Primary Value** of your business is delivered,
> =OR=
> Where you **Regularly Meet** with customers or prospects,
> =OR=
> Where the primary **Administration or Management** of your business is conducted.

Almost everyone operating a legitimate business from their home can qualify under option #3.

Although the Home Office is just one of the many elements in computing the Business Use Percentage of your home, let's start with that one.

Option 1:

Measure to get the square footage of each 'finished' area in your home.

Add up all of those areas.

Divide that total into the square footage of the home-office.

The result is your BUP.

Option 2, provided by an "IRS Clarification:"

In a "clarification," the IRS said "If all rooms of the home are approximately the same size, and if one of those rooms is used regularly and exclusively for business purposes, the taxpayer may use the percentage of the number of rooms used, to calculate the BUP." – i.e., you have five rooms in your home, and one is used as a home-office, you can claim 20% as your BUP without doing any measurements.

Let's look at the <u>significance</u> of that "clarification."

No one has a bathroom "approximately the same size" as their living room, or a closet "approximately the same size" as their den, or a foyer "approximately the same size" as the dining room, so the only logical way a reasonable person could interpret that IRS wording is: in calculating BUP by any reasonable method, one is not expected to include the floor space of closets, bathrooms, foyers, hallways, stairways, pantries, laundry rooms, etc.

That having been said, look back at Option 1, described earlier. When measuring square footage of "finished areas of the home, you may want to include *only* "primary" rooms in determining your "total square footage," and then divide that number into the business use total.

About those word, "business use total…" The areas of your home used "regularly and exclusively" for business may include areas not within the home-office. In fact, the tax form you use to claim the deduction is Form 8829, named "Expenses for Business Use of Your Home," *not* home-office.

If you have bookcases in your living room or den containing **only** business related books, your BUP calculations can include the square footage occupied by that bookcase -- *plus* "a reasonable amount of walking space around it!" (Of course, the bookcase itself may also be a tax-deductible Business Asset, as we will discuss soon.)

If you have a "conference table" in a section of your den which is used "regularly and exclusively" for meeting with customers or clients, then you could also include the square footage occupied by the table and the chairs around it (plus walking space around it) in your BUP calculations.

Now, what if you also need to store business products (and **only** business products) in one side of a closet and hang your out-of-season clothes in the other side, or place a business-use-only copy machine in a hallway? Again, the space occupied by half of the closet and the copy machine (plus "a reasonable walking space around it"), can be <u>added</u> to your BUP calculations.

Remember, "exclusive use" areas do not have to be bound by walls or other partitions. They can simply be portions of rooms that are used <u>only for business purposes</u>.

So, no matter where your business-use-only equipment best "fits" in your home, the area it occupies can be included in your BUP calculations.

Summary: You can include 100% of the square footage of your exclusive-use home-office in your BUP, <u>plus the exclusive-use *areas* of other rooms.</u>

If your Business Use Percentage (BUP) ends up being 15%, for example, your indirect expenses are calculated at that rate.

Imagine that! Legally deducting 15% of the cost of your home heating and cooling bill, 15% of your rent cost **(yes, RENT, not just mortgage interest!)**, 15% of your home maintenance and upkeep costs, etc.! **[IRS Publication 587]**

Here is an 'extreme' (but real) example…

If a professional wedding photographer displays his photographs ("product samples") throughout his home, he or she could have a very high BUP. How's that?

When an engaged couple visits the photographer's place of business (in his home, of course!), thinking they may want this photographer to photograph their wedding, and they ask to see examples of his previous work, guess what he does?

Instead of handing them a photo album, he takes them on a tour of his home, of course, where examples of his work are framed and hanging on most of the walls! He may have legitimately converted a very large portion of his home into "product display areas."

> **NOTE:** If an "extreme example" such as the above applies to you, be sure to consult with an experienced pro who specializes in home business tax law.

You could potentially write-off the majority of the square footage of more than one room in your house, if using each of them is "reasonable and necessary."   **[IRC Section 280 A]**

Let's look at another example…

Do you have a formal dining room in your home? If so, how often do you use it? Never? (Dusting the furniture in there in Saturdays doesn't count as "using it.")

If that's the case with you, then perhaps you "re-label" your dining room as an additional room that you use <u>regularly</u> and <u>exclusively</u> for business purposes.

Let's say you "regularly and exclusively" use that room to…

- Assemble mailings to your customers/prospects
- Process your invoices and payments, and to fill out deposit slips
- Store 'samples' and products that you sell
- Create your marketing plans, etc.

Be sure you use the room on a <u>regular basis</u> (not just occasionally) and <u>exclusively</u> (not just most of the time) in order to keep from invalidating your deduction under the "Exclusive Use Rule."

NOTE:

If you use a dining room, for example, it would be a good idea to take some photos that clearly shows the business use, and place copies of the photos in your tax file.

Let your business **e—x—p—a—n—d** to encompass as much of your home as is Necessary and Reasonable. Can you see why a small home would probably have a much higher Business Use Percentage than a mansion? The business-use *square footage* may be larger in a mansion, but the business-use *percentage* would likely be lower.

How about the non-finished square footage? Let's say you store business products, inventory and supplies in the loft of your barn. Under these circumstances, what's another term you might use for the 'loft?' How about "warehouse?" Maintenance and upkeep of a business warehouse or storage area is tax-deductible. Not the whole 100%, of course, but a "reasonable percentage."

What if the barn needs repairs and repainting? The percentage of the barn that is used exclusively for business purposes (storage, in this case), can be applied to the repair and maintenance expenses, as a business tax deduction.

[IRS IRC Section § 280 A(c)(2)]

Keep thinking like a business owner who rents space in an office building. Your 'office building' just happens to be your home.

> **Disclaimer: These are just examples for illustration purposes. Do not claim these (or any other) deductions without the advice of a tax professional who specializes in home-business tax law.**

You might want to provide your tax professional with a sketch of each business-use room of your home, including dimensions of the rooms themselves and dimensions of the business-use areas within them, along with the total square footage of your home. Your tax pro can then help you compute your BUP, and also the depreciation you could claim for your Business Assets (which we will discuss soon). Then keep this sketch in your tax file in case of a future audit.

DIRECT Expenses:

Direct Expenses are expenses directly related to the conduct of your business. This category would include office supplies; telephone service; necessary media subscriptions; perhaps cellular phones, beepers and pagers; employee benefits; repairs and upkeep of exclusive use areas; and professional dues and memberships. Direct expenses generally are 100% deductible.

There is One Important Exception to "Direct Expense" Deductions

The rules about deductibility of your **telephone bill** are a little bit different.

[IRS Publication 587]

Your **base** phone charges are **not** tax deductible, **period**. "Base phone charge" refers to the amount you would pay if you had no long distance calls, no second line, no add-on services like call waiting, call forwarding, caller ID, 3-way calling, etc. The cost of minimal phone service = your "base phone cost."

This "base phone cost" exclusion applies only to the first "land-line" in your home. Any additional lines may be 100% deductible if they are used only for business purposes (such as a dedicated fax line, for example).

Even though your "base phone cost" is not deductible, your "add-on" services could be 100% deductible if subscribing to them is "ordinary and necessary" for your business.

If you get an itemized phone bill, you would annotate every long-distance as either a business call ("B") or a personal call ("P"). If the primary purpose of a call is to discuss business, and "personal chat" is secondary, the call may still be deductible.

If you have "flat rate" long distance service, and if the reason you subscribe to flat rate is because you make a large number of long distance *business* calls, then 100% of your flat-rate bill could be deductible. Occasionally calling your sister would have no affect whatsoever on the amount of your phone bill, so the cost should still be 100% deductible.

BUSINESS ASSETS:

As you would expect, Business Assets include **equipment** such as computers, fax machines, etc.; and **furniture** such as desks, desk chairs, and filing cabinets. These assets are depreciable at 100%, providing they are used exclusively for business purposes.

Thanks to the "Jobs Growth and Tax Reconciliation Act" you now have an "accelerated depreciation" option. Under a "Section 179 Election," you can *immediately* depreciate the *entire* business use percentage amount of new or used business assets you purchase in 2009 (as long as business use is at least

51%) up to $250,000, *this year*, rather than depreciating the item over 5 or 7 years. (In Chapter Eight we'll discuss how this applies to vehicles purchased for business use). The amount of this deduction is limited by the amount of profit from your home-based business.

Now, what about assets used *partially* for business purposes, but *not exclusively*? If customers, clients and/or prospects visit your place of business (your home) regularly and frequently, it would be customary to furnish a lobby (your living room?) and perhaps a meeting room (maybe your den?), and to have equipment available for making business presentations (TV and DVD, for example).

The furniture and equipment in these rooms also are tax deductible, although not at a full 100%, because they too, are only partially used as Business Assets. So, exactly how much can you deduct?

Let's say (based on your day planner records or upon an "actual-use-log"), your sofa is used 3 out of every 10 times for business purposes, and 7 out of every 10 times for personal, family use. You would likely be allowed to deduct 30% of the cost of the sofa as a **Business Asset**.

What Happens When You
SELL YOUR HOME
That Contained a Home-Based Business?

Good news for home-business owners! A recent change IRS regulations now state that there will no longer be taxation on the 'gain on sale' (i.e., profit) portion of a principal residence that would be allocated to the business use of that residence.

Since you were <u>authorized</u> to claim a business deduction for depreciation of the portion of your home used exclusively for business, a 'recapture' of the depreciation taken for home office will likely be required, <u>even if you did not claim it</u>, but that amount is miniscule compared to what taxation on the 'gain' could have meant. Be sure to consult with a tax professional if this situation applies to you.

You Can Even Write-off Your RENT!

Yes, it is true! As we said earlier, when you have a home-based business, you can legally deduct the Business Use Percentage of **either** your mortgage interest **OR** the BUP of your **RENT**.

Does a "traditional business" have to <u>own</u> its office space in order to deduct the cost of using it? Of course not, so why should you?

Since your home is your place of business, it does not matter whether you own or rent your "office space." You can deduct the "Business Use Percentage" of your mortgage interest <u>or your rent payments</u>, *either one!*

Finally, for profitable businesses, *renters* can get the same tax deductions as their home-buyer friends!

Is this a great country, or what?

Also Deduct Business Publications, Cleaning Services, and Much More!

Yes, again, it's true! If reading certain newspapers and magazines is ordinary and necessary for running your type of home-based business, which is highly probable, they could be tax deductible business expenses, just as they are for businesses based in office buildings.

Also, a traditional business can deduct the costs of janitorial service, and likewise, the owner of a home-based business can deduct house cleaning expenses for the business-use portions of the home.

Does a **traditional** business get to write-off the costs of repairs, general maintenance, trash collection, etc.?   Of course. Well, if the "business use percentage" of your home is 15%, for example, **you** get to write-off 15% of **your** repairs, general maintenance, driveway resurfacing, snow removal, trash collection, etc.

Hold On, We Have Barely Begun Saving You Money on Your Taxes!

You are about to learn some tax information your current tax preparer probably hasn't even thought about – unless he or she is a seasoned expert in home-business tax-law. (That's why we are even citing the sources to prove it!)

If you find this information amazing, just wait until you read the rest of this tax-reduction guide.

Pull out a pencil and calculator and let's see how much of YOUR current expenses could become tax-deductible…

Typical Home-Based Business Expenses

Calculating Your "Business Use Percentage" (BUP)

1. Total finished square feet of your home =   A: _____
2. Total sq. ft. used <u>exclusively</u> in your business =   B: _____
3. B ÷ A =   BUP: _____%

Estimating Your Tax Deductions

Expense Category	Annual Cost	Conversion Factor	Estimated Tax Deduction
Mortgage or Rent	$_____	x BUP%	$_____
Gas	$_____	x BUP%	$_____
Electric	$_____	x BUP%	$_____
Water/Sewer	$_____	x BUP%	$_____
Trash Collection	$_____	x BUP%	$_____
House Cleaning	$_____	x BUP%	$_____
Deck Treatment	$_____	x BUP%	$_____
Driveway Repairs	$_____	x BUP%	$_____
Security Alarm	$_____	x BUP%	$_____
Repairs/Maintenance	$_____	x BUP%	$_____
Business Supplies	$_____	x 100%	$_____
Postage and Courier	$_____	x 100%	$_____
Subscriptions	$_____	x 100%	$_____
Cards and Stamps	$_____	x 100%	$_____
Internet Access Fees	$_____	x 100%	$_____
Books/Magazines	$_____	x 100%	$_____
Phone Bills**	$_____	x 100%	$_____
Asset Purchases***	$_____	x 100%	$_____
Depreciable Assets	$_____	x 14.28%	$_____
Other	$_____	x ??%	$_____

▼ ▼

Current Expenses = $_____

Estimated Business Deductions = $_____

** Excluding "base amount" for first phone line.
*** Maximum deduction is $250,000 for 2009

There Are <u>Dollar-Amount Limits</u> on SOME of these Deductions

Deductions for expenses falling into the *INdirect* Expense category (rent, utilities, repairs, maintenance, etc.) are limited by the amount of net income (profits) of your home-based business in any particular year.

HOWEVER, you never lose these Indirect Expense deductions because they can be carried-forward for use in **any** future profitable year.

For example, if your home-based business earned a profit of $4,000 last year after all other expenses and deductions are applied, your total INdirect Expense deductions on last year's Tax Return would be capped at $4,000.

If you qualified for $9,000 in indirect expenses deductions last year, but were able to claim only $4,000 worth, you can "carry forward" the entire remaining $5,000 worth of deductions for use *in any future year.*

In addition, you never lose the full amount of your mortgage interest and property tax deductions if you itemize. In fact, it is possible that these two items could be deductible to you on a Schedule A, even if you have a business loss.

Deductions for all **other** expense categories generally **are** allowed to exceed the amount of net income generated by your home business, and usually be applied against <u>ALL other income sources</u>, including interest, dividends, rental properties, W-2 and 1099 income, and more.

Is your tax pro Saving you money, or Costing you money? Download a special Report by that title at www.HomeBusinessTaxSavings.com in the Resource Center section.

CHAPTER FIVE

How to Write-Off
Furniture and Equipment
Used Totally or Partially for Business

As mentioned in the last chapter, a business in an office building would be expected to have a sofa, coffee table, lamps, etc. in its lobby for the use of customers and prospects visiting the office, right?

You've already discovered that if you meet customers and prospects in your home, you have the same tax deduction rights, although you have to pro rate the amount based on business usage.

Let's use a sofa for our example. You could either convert a currently-owned sofa from Personal Use to Partial Business Use or you could acquire a new sofa as a Partial Business Asset.

For "converting," the calculation goes like this...

First you determine the approximate value of your sofa at the time of conversion. Then you determine the percentage of business-use versus personal use of the sofa. Next you multiply the value, times the percentage for business-use. Divide the resulting number by seven, and that is the amount you can depreciate each year for seven years, beginning this year.

An example may help to clarify...

Let's say your sofa was purchased new for $1,000, and today it's worth about $700. And let's say out of every 10 times the sofa is used, 6 are for business and 4 are for personal use (thus, business use = 60%). Next you multiply $700 by 60%, and the result is $420. Now, since you are required to depreciate the "asset" over a 7-year period, you can claim 1/7th of $420 (which is $60) on each of your next seven tax returns as Asset Depreciation.

The process of depreciation is somewhat different when you **buy** a sofa for partial business use, rather than **converting one** from Personal use to Business use. By the way, it doesn't matter whether you purchase a new sofa or a used sofa – as long as it is "new to you."

After your business is established, if you bought that same sofa for $1,000 (whether it was new or used), Uncle Sam actually gives you a choice of two methods you can use to get your tax benefits.

1. You can choose to multiply the $1,000 by your 60% business-use (which = $600), and then depreciate that $600 amount over seven years. (Same as in the example above, except in this case you get a $85+/year deduction for Asset Depreciation instead of only $60/year.)

- OR -

2. You can choose to deduct the entire 60% of the $1,000 purchase (which = $600) ALL in the same tax year in which it was purchased, in most cases. It must have been purchased "for use at least 51% in your business." The amount deducted cannot exceed your total earned income ("profit") in the year of purchase.

If you need tax deductions this year, you might choose the second option, but if you do not need the deductions this year, the first option might be a better decision. Be sure to consult with your tax professional **before** purchasing **any** asset that will be used in your business.

Note: The depreciation period is only FIVE years for electronic equipment (classified for tax purposes as "listed property") **such as:**

- Computers and peripherals
- Phones and phone systems
- TVs, DVD players, tape players, CD players
- Photo-copiers, fax machines, scanners and printers

[IRC Sec 280F(d)(4)(A)]

Items of furniture or equipment which cost less than a few hundred dollars may be considered as "supplies" and thus, written-off as Business *Supplies* rather than Business *Assets*, and not subject to the multi-year depreciation rules that apply to business equipment and furniture.

For example, if you purchase a filing cabinet for $200, you do not have to depreciate it over a 7-year period, or if you purchase a new calculator for $100 you do not have to depreciate it over 5-years.

Assets and Supplies in the Exclusive Use Areas

Of course, the assets (equipment, desks, chairs, etc.) and the supplies (items worth less than a few hundred dollars) in your exclusive-use home-office, and other such area of the home, are 100% depreciable, whether they were purchased before you went into business (converted assets and supplies) or after you went into business (newly acquired assets).

A key point is that assets (new or used) purchased and placed into service when or after you go into business may qualify for "accelerated depreciation" under the Section 179 Expense Election, which means that you can deduct the entire BUP of the asset cost (because it will be used 100% for business) whether it is totally paid for or financed (up to $250,000 in 2009).

[Jobs Growth and Tax Reconciliation Act]

CHAPTER SIX

HIRE Your KIDS
and get some HUGE Benefits!

When you are a sole-proprietor, hiring employees presents you with a few more obligations, but if your employees are immediate family members, it can mean huge new tax deductions.

There are NO withholding requirements for employees who are minors under 18 years of age. Your obligations include withholding payroll taxes and filing quarterly and annual tax forms for any employees 18 years or older.   But those requirements are minor compared to the additional tax benefits you can qualify for.

HIRE your KIDS --
Don't Pay Them an *Allowance*!

It is quite common to see children actively involved in the family business. Even young children can perform valuable services that are "reasonable and customary" for most any type of business. Many entrepreneurs, however, miss out on some major tax savings available for hiring their children to work in their home-business – simply because they don't know the rules and benefits you are about to discover.

[Tax Court Memo 1992-50 in Jordan v IRS Commissioner]

The wage *expenses* are <u>tax-deductible</u> to you, and the wage *income* is usually <u>tax-free</u> to your child (more on this below.)

[Reg. Sec 1.162-7(a)]

The federal tax-free limit on earned income for dependent children is $5,700 per child for 2010. (The amount is equal to the Standard Deduction, which changes each year.)

[Rev. Proc. 95-53 and IRC Section 63(h)(2)]

If they earn *more than* the $5,700 tax-free amount, they'll simply pay the minimum (currently 10%) tax rate on any amount over and above $5,700.

In addition they can earn and contribute up to $4,000 in a Roth IRA per year. They will pay taxes on the $4,000 (but at the minimum 10% rate), but no taxes will be due when they withdraw the money for retirement.

Most states follow the federal guidelines on tax-free income for dependents, however, earnings of a minor may be subject to a local payroll tax, depending on where you live. Be sure to check with your professional tax advisor to be certain that you are complying with all state and local tax laws.

In order for you to employ *anyone*, you should have an Employer Identification Number (EIN), which is issued by the IRS at no cost.

> **The EIN Application, Form SS-4, is available as a free download in the "Resource Center" at www.HomeBusinessTaxSavings.com** or from the official IRS web site, www.IRS.gov

Other requirements for hiring minor children are <u>easy</u>, but <u>specific</u>.

1. You should have a <u>signed *Employment Agreement*</u> in order to establish a *bone fide* employer-employee relationship, and for documenting hiring date, assigned duties, agreed-upon wage level and payday schedule.

2. File Form I-9 to *<u>verify work eligibility</u>*.

3. File Form W-4 to determine *<u>withholding requirements</u>* and verify the employee's Social Security Number

4. The type of work must be *<u>ordinary and necessary</u>* for your type of business.

5. Document that the *services were <u>actually performed</u>* (timesheets or work log).

6. The *wage level must be <u>reasonable</u>* for the services actually rendered and the age of the child.

7. <u>Wages</u> must be *<u>paid on a consistent and timely basis</u>* (at least monthly).

8. <u>Document</u> that the wages *<u>were actually paid</u>* (always use a business check).

9.   *File Forms W-2 and W-3* **at the end of the year, documenting wages paid.**

Can you employ *young* children? The Federal Tax Court has ruled that **children as young as six years old** can qualify as employees of their parents' sole proprietorship or LLC business.

[Eller v. Commissioner, 77 T.C. 934 (1981)]

When determining the scope of work to be included in the Employment Agreement, be aware of Tax Court rulings that said the services performed should *not* be those that would reasonably called household chores, because "they are part of parental training and discipline rather than services rendered by an employee for an employer."

NOTE:

There may be quarterly or annual state / local withholding required depending upon where you live, but there is no Federal withholding for Dependents under 18 years old.

[Denman v. Commissioner, 48 TC 439]

[Hable v. Commissioner, 48 TCM 1079]

Another court case sheds more light: "Ensure that the duties are necessary for the operation of the business and that, if these services had not been performed by the employed children, a third party would have had to be hired."

[Eller v. Commissioner, 77 TC 934]

If they are your own children, are under 18 years old, and qualify as Dependents on your tax return, they are exempt from payroll taxes, and the business is not required to withhold or to pay Social Security or Medicare taxes on wages paid to those children. If you have children between 18 and 24, they may also qualify for the $5,700 exclusion IF they if they are full-time students at least 5 months during the tax year, although they will be subject to payroll tax withholding.

[IRC Section 3121(b)(3)(A) and § 3306(c)(5)]

[Tax Court Ruling 48 TC 439, 450 (196) in Denman v. Commissioner]

In order to bullet-proof this category of your home-business deductions, start by writing a formal Employment Agreement. This will document that a bona fide employer-employee relationship exists, and state the hiring date, wage level, work to be performed and payday schedule.

> **A fill-in-the-blanks Employment Agreement is available for download in the Resource Center at www.HomeBusinessTaxSavings.**

The wage rate you pay each child must be reasonable within your region of the country, within your type of business, and appropriate for the age of the child.

[Revenue Ruling 73-393]

How do you establish what is "reasonable?" One way would be to get an outside resource, or third party, to give you a written estimate for the work to be performed. Put a copy in your tax file, and then pay your family member the equivalent of that amount, or a little less.

[Rev. Rul. 72-23, 1972-1 C.B. 43]

Or you could determine what a reasonable person might pay a small business, freelancer or independent contractor for such services, and pay a similar or lower wage to your family member.

[IRS Regulation § 1.162-7(a)]

NOTE: Before hiring your children, be sure to check with your home-business tax advisor to be sure your all of your documentation and reporting will comply with IRS rules.

The kids (as employees) have to document what work they did to earn the money **[Revenue Ruling 73-393]** so have them fill out a simple "work log" with headings like:

- Date they worked
- Type of work performed
- Amount of time spent working

Have them initial each entry, and submit it to you for approval. (You "approve" it by putting your initial next to theirs.)

Pay Attention Here, because…

You're about to discover how you could pay for …

- The **car** your high-schooler wants
- Designer-label **clothes** the kids 'require'
- **Movie and Concert tickets**
- A High School **graduation trip**
- **College tuition**, books and supplies
- Your daughter's expensive **wedding**

...ALL in *TAX-FREE* Dollars!

Here's how...

The $5,700/year Uncle Sam lets your children earn tax-free as employees (in 2010), is equivalent to about $110.00 per week, for a 52-week year!

Now, you're saying, "Who gives their kids 110 dollars a week in allowance?" Maybe nobody does in "allowance," but YOU may in "wages!" And here's why...

Let's say you employ your child to perform ongoing work in your home-based business, and agree to pay him or her $75 per week for those services. Assuming they have turned in their "work logs," on payday, you pay them their weekly wages – always with a business check.

You'll want to open a separate checking, savings or investment account for each child to deposit their payroll checks. The bank or other financial institution will require it to be a "custodial account," since minors cannot legally conduct banking transactions. That means **only <u>you</u> (the account**

'custodian') will be authorized to make deposits or withdrawals on that account, since the child is under-age.

For recordkeeping purposes, you should deposit ALL of their paychecks into that account. (Make sure it's an interest-bearing account -- you will see why in a minute.) You may wish to go to the bank *with your child* to make the deposits and make any withdrawals. Why? If they are young, they may learn for the first time that they have to put money IN the bank before getting money OUT of the bank. How many kids have grown up thinking that adults can get money anytime they want, if they just insert a plastic card into the slot of a bank machine?

Reader Alert!

Here is Where It Gets REALLY Interesting…

The law requires you to **pay them** the amount they **earned**, in order for you to be able to deduct the wage as a business expense.

BUT . . .

There is very little restriction on how you (as his/her account custodian) can <u>use</u> the money after it has been paid, as long as it is used to directly benefit the child.

[Revenue Ruling 73-393]

These funds might be used to help pay for private school tuition, after school sports equipment, music lessons or instruments, school trips, educational summer camps – even sox and underwear!

You might decide to simply tell your child,

"You may withdraw $10 (for example) out of each week's pay, to spend any way you wish; however, the other $65.00 will stay in the (interest-bearing) account to be used to pay for your_____."

Fill in the blank with whatever you like -- perhaps one of the examples above, or maybe new clothes, college tuition, wedding, graduation trip, car, etc.

Did you ever, in your wildest dreams, anticipate that you would be able to pay for school supplies and tennis shoes, or pay for cars, trips and weddings, out of *non-taxed* dollars? **It's true! It's real! And it's 100% legal!**

There are other practical "learning-lesson" benefits to this strategy that are at least as important as the tax benefits.

By working for you, the child learns that, as an employee, there are only two ways to earn more money, and both of them require permission of the employer.

One way, as an hourly employee, is to work more hours. The lesson: If the boss agrees, you can earn more money – by working harder!

The other way to earn more money as a salaried employee, is to perform work that has a higher perceived value than what you're doing now. The lesson: No employee is ever paid what he/she is worth, only what the job is worth – and the boss decides what the job is worth.

Your child will also begin learning the value of money, and the trade-offs between spending and saving money, and between instant-gratification and delayed-gratification.

Imagine being in a store with your child to buy a new pair of shoes. The child wants the $150 'designer-label' shoes; you prefer the $45 'generic' brand. Perhaps you offer to pay $45, but tell them that anything over that amount will come out of their checking/savings account. Perhaps you let the child choose, knowing that whatever they have left in their checking/savings account will be theirs when they turn 18.

Here's my favorite: If they contributed the maximum of $4,000 per year into a Roth IRA <u>for just five years</u>, say from ages 16 through 21, and if that money earned an average of 10% APR, by the time they reach retirement age 65, they'd have MORE THAN $2-MILLION in their account. They'd pay taxes when they put the money in, but only at the 10% *minimum tax rate*. But they pay NO TAXES when they withdraw it.

Isn't that a great tax-savings strategy *and* a great learning opportunity for your children?

CHAPTER SEVEN

HIRE Your SPOUSE
and deduct
ALL out-of-pocket Health Costs
for the Whole Family!

Non-reimbursed health care costs (money you spend out of your own pocket, and not reimbursed by health insurance) is becoming a major factor in our household budgets, even for people who have health insurance.

Why? Health insurance companies can't drive their premiums much higher, or they'll lose even more of their members, so what are they doing instead? Many are beginning to move many types of procedures from the list of "covered expenses" to "non-covered/excluded." Consider orthodontics – braces. The cost was routinely covered by most health care plans, but some are now dropping the benefit altogether. Why? Cost.

From the time you or your child walks into an orthodontist's office for the first time for an exam, until the last time when the braces are removed, the total cost will most likely be in the range of $3,000 to $6,000. Today, instead of being responsible only for co-pays, you may be on the hook for the full amount, paid out of your own pocket, with zero help from your health insurance company.

It's not just orthodontic procedures that are dropping off the "covered benefits" list. Take a look at your own coverage and you may see that it no longer includes chiropractic, elective procedures (such as Lasik), medical devices (such as hearing aids), vision wear (such as contact lenses), etc., etc.

Aren't health care expenses Tax-Deductible?

Without a home based business, most taxpayers must jump through two hoops in order to deduct out-of-pocket health expenses.

FIRST, *they must itemize* their tax deductions, because health expenses are claimed on Schedule A (schedule of itemized deductions). If they don't file a Schedule A, they don't get to claim any health expenses.

SECOND, even if they DO file a Schedule A, the amount they can claim is limited to the amount above 7.5% of their taxable income. Example: If your income is $50,000, the first $3,750 (7.5%) of their medical costs are not deductible – only the amount above that can be claimed on Schedule A!

They are responsible for the first $3,750, which they will pay in after-tax dollars. In order to pay $3,750 for *any* non-deductible expense of *any* kind, they would have to earn more than $5,000 in wages, in order to bring home $3,750 in take-home pay.

That's a Problem!

But YOU are Sitting on the ANSWER!

If you hire your spouse to work in your home-business, he/she becomes an *employee*, right? Employees may receive "Employee Benefits." Who determines what benefits are offered to employees? The *employer*, of course. Oh, that's you! Where are we going with this?

The **cost** of Employee Benefits is **deductible** to the **employer** as a business expense. The **value** of the benefits received, is **tax free** to the **employee**.

[IRC Section § 162(a)]

The valuable Benefit you/employer offer to your spouse/employee, is a "Self-Insured Medical Reimbursement Plan (MRP)."

The MRP Benefit (which is a legal Employee Benefits document) states that the employer will reimburse the employee for all out-of-pocket health related expenses incurred by the employee and all member of his/her immediate family. (Ummm, that includes you and the kids!)

What just happened? You just found a legal way to get a **tax deduction for every penny of health-related expenses for yourself and all members of your immediate family**. And you have no requirement to file a Schedule A and no 7.5% threshold to overcome. It's called a *"Section 105 Plan"* because that's the Section of the Tax Code that authorizes it.

The Tax Court said: "Such medical coverage is a common business Expense and is deductible by self-employed persons the same way it is by other businesses."

[Ralph E. Frahm, TC Memo 2007-351]

Steps to Hiring Your Spouse...

You will be expected to be able to prove that a bona fide employer/employee relationship exists between you and your spouse. The feds defines it this way: "The first spouse substantially controls the business in terms of management decisions, and the second spouse is under the direction and control of the first spouse."

NOTE: If spouses carry on the business together and share in the profits and losses, they may be considered as Partners in a Partnership whether or not they have a formal Partnership Agreement.

If you already you have an EIN, you do not need another one. Each business (including sole proprietors) need only one.

> **If you already you have an EIN, you do not need another one. Each business (including sole proprietors) need only one. The EIN Application, Form SS 4, is available as a free download from www.HomeBusinessTaxSavings.com (in "Resource Center") or from the IRS web site, www.IRS.gov**

Here are the steps to doing it right.

Do not skip ANY of these steps, or you could risk losing this huge benefit.

1. **You should have a <u>signed *Employment Agreement*</u> to document that a *bone fide* employer-employee relationship exists, and to document hiring date, assigned duties, agreed-upon wage level and payday schedule.**

2. **The type of work must be <u>*Ordinary And Necessary*</u> for your business type.** Specified duties may *not* include "domestic chores normally associated with husband-wife relationship".

3. **Document that the services were <u>*Actually Performed.*</u>**

4. **The <u>*pay must be Reasonable*</u> for the services actually rendered.**

5. **Wages must be paid on a <u>*Consistent And Timely Basis*</u> (at *least* monthly).**

6. **<u>Document</u> that those <u>*Wages Were Actually Paid*</u> (use a business check).**

For all ADULT Employees you must ALSO:

7. File Form I-9 to *verify work eligibility*.

8. File Form W-4 to determine *withholding requirements* and verify the employee's Social Security Number.

9. *Withhold Social Security & Medicare* taxes from wages (but not FUTA, unemployment taxes, which are exempt).

    NOTE: Wages are taxed at 15.3% for Social Security and Medicare combined. The employee pays 7.65%, and the employer pays a matching amount. Self-employed persons pay the full 15.3% on all earnings as a sole proprietor or under an LLC.

10. File Forms W-2 and W-3 at the end of the year, documenting wages paid.

11. File a Form 941 quarterly or Form 944 annually,

12. File Forms W-2 and 940 (or 944) at the end of the year.

There may also be state and local reporting requirements, depending on where you live.

NOTE: The services performed must be for duties performed as an *employee* not for "domestic duties" normally performed by family members living in the same home.

> NOTE: If you do not understand the process of filing quarterly Form 941s and annual Forms 940, 944 and W-2 see Employee Payroll Service under Resource Center at www.HomeBusinessTaxSavings.com

NOW, you are ready to Establish this <u>Employee Benefit</u> as "Official Company Policy"

"All employees, **and their spouses and dependents**, will be reimbursed for all health-related expenses that are not reimbursed under any other Insurance Plan."

A WORD OF CAUTION:

Only establish this company policy if your business will be hiring only your own family members. If you establish this policy and then hire non-family members, you may be required to offer the benefit to them as well, and that may defeat the

Therefore, your entire family would become covered under this Employee Benefit.

By the way, this also covers many of the costs of weight loss programs if prescribed by a licensed medical practitioner, and the cost of nutritional supplements if prescribed or recommended (in writing) for treatment or prevention of a specific health condition.

[Pub 535, p 56]

This MRP allows you to legally deduct ALL insurance plan annual deductibles, co-pays for doctor visits and prescription drugs, plus 'non-covered' expenses like orthodontics, eyeglasses, contact lenses, dental work, chiropractic visits, and even many drugstore purchases.

[Reg Sec 71-588; Plr. 9409006]

Even nutritional supplements, vitamins, herbs, and "natural remedies," etc. <u>*may*</u> be included as health care expenses **IF** a licensed (in your state)

medical health care provider has declared them to be a "medical necessity" and recommended them (get it in writing) for "treating <u>or preventing</u> specific health conditions." **[IRS Pub 502, p 15]**

No minimum thresholds apply; every single dollar is tax-deductible by the business as an employee benefit cost.

It is important that this "Employee Benefit" be established <u>in writing</u>, as a <u>legal document</u>, and that the Benefit is reasonable in relation to the level of services the employee provides to your business. **[Reg Sec 1.105-5(a)]**

A fill-in-the-blanks version of a Self-Insured Medical Cost Reimbursement Plan is available for download from www.HomeBusinessTaxSavings.com

---

A Word About the Level of Your Spouse's Wages

Since Social Security and Medicare payroll taxes are calculated based on a *percentage* of the employee's wages, the lower the wage level, the lower the dollar amount of taxes.

Therefore, you may want to stay on the conservative side of "reasonable wage level," in order to minimize the taxes you'll be required to pay.

Even if you employ your spouse at "minimum wage," you qualify to use this medical expense reimbursement tax strategy, so long as this benefit is reasonable in relation to the level of services provided by your spouse.

[IRC § 3306(c)(5); IRS Pub 15, and IRS Circular E apply]

In order to be considered *Bone Fide* Employees,

How Many Hours Do They Need to Work?

The answer is not crystal clear, but it appears to be approximately two hours a week, or 100 hours/year. Here's what it says in various authoritative sources:

Temp Reg §1.469-1T(g)(3)(i):

This IRS Regulation states that an employee must work **at least 100 hours per year** in order to satisfy the guidelines for "Significant Participation."

2001 FED ¶21.965:

"*Material* Participation Guidelines" requires employees to meet <u>ONE</u> of these TWO requirements in order to comply with "Passive Loss Rules"

1. Work more than 500 hours/year (about 10 hours/week),

OR

2. Work more than 100 hours/year AND this level of activity is *not less than* any *other* employee.

NOTE: If your Employment Agreement for hiring family members specifies working requirements that fall short of the above guidelines, you should first consult a tax professional who specializes in home-business tax law, to ensure that your employment arrangement is IRS-compliant.

> **An Employment Agreement with family member employees is an important legal document that substantiates that a bona fide Employer Employee relationship exists, and specifies the agreed upon type of work, wage/salary level, and payroll schedule. You can download a fill-in-the-blanks Employment Agreement at www.HomeBusinessTaxSavings.com**

CHAPTER EIGHT

The Key to Your Largest Single Tax-Deduction May be in Your IGNITION!

Your car, whether you own or lease, probably represents your third-largest monthly expense, coming in right behind **taxes** and your **mortgage** or **rent**.

In all likelihood, however, **your car** also represents **your largest single source of potential tax-savings**. So, finding a way to legally write-off a significant portion of your automobile costs, represents a major tax-savings opportunity for you, potentially worth thousands of dollars in new, legal tax deductions. **[IRS Temp. Reg. § 1.274-5T(b)(6)(1)(B)]**

Many eligible taxpayers skip over this deduction, just because they think the recordkeeping is too difficult and isn't worth it. *Little do they know…*

If you usually use the same personal vehicle for all of your business use, the IRS requires that you maintain a vehicle-use log **for only 90 days** and yet you get tax deductions for the entire year. Since 90 days is one-fourth of a year, if you keep a log for "*a typical 90-consecutive day period*" (Tax Code wording) all the numbers collected during the 90 days, may be multiplied by 4, to produce your <u>annual numbers</u>. How easy is that?

[Temp. Treas. Reg. § 1.274-5T(c)(3)(ii)(C), Ex. (1)]

And that 90-day recordkeeping "task" can be reduced to doing just one simple thing each time you slip behind the wheel, and it *literally* takes about as little time as it takes to fasten your seat belt.

Simply keep a Vehicle-Use Log handy in your car, and – *for only 90 consecutive days* -- <u>each time you put the key in your ignition</u>, you simply answer four questions:

- **What <u>day</u> is it?**   **(Date)**
- **<u>Where</u> am I going?**   **(Destination)**

- **<u>Why</u> am I going there?**   **(Primary Purpose)**
- **How <u>far away</u> is it?**   **(Miles traveled)**

Example:

Date:	Destination:	Primary Purpose	Miles
01/11/10	Joe's Coffee Shop	Business Presentation to Jan Kelly	12
01/12/10	Bank	Business Deposit	6
01/13/10	(Personal)	(Personal)	5
01/13/10	Post Office	Buy Business Postage	5

That's it. And by the way, Destination does not need to be precise. For example, under the heading Destination, you do not need the address of "Joe's Coffee Shop."

Then just enter your odometer readings and/or total miles traveled.

[IRC Section § 274(d)]

How long could that take? I'd guess about 5-10 seconds, and only for 90 days!

A Vehicle-Use Log <u>which you are free to reproduce</u> for your own use, is provided on the next page.

To download the 2010 Vehicle Use Log visit www.HomeBusinessTaxSavings.com and click on Free Downloads under the "Resource Center" tab.

2010 Vehicle Use Log

Date	Starting Odometer Reading	Ending Odometer Reading	Total Miles Traveled	Expenses Incurred (gas, tolls, etc.)

Destination:		Primary Purpose of Trip:	

Date	Starting Odometer Reading	Ending Odometer Reading	Total Miles Traveled	Expenses Incurred (gas, tolls, etc.)

Destination:		Primary Purpose of Trip:	

Date	Starting Odometer Reading	Ending Odometer Reading	Total Miles Traveled	Expenses Incurred (gas, tolls, etc.)

Destination:		Primary Purpose of Trip:	

Date	Starting Odometer Reading	Ending Odometer Reading	Total Miles Traveled	Expenses Incurred (gas, tolls, etc.)

Destination:		Primary Purpose of Trip:	

Date	Starting Odometer Reading	Ending Odometer Reading	Total Miles Traveled	Expenses Incurred (gas, tolls, etc.)

Destination:		Primary Purpose of Trip:	

Date	Starting Odometer Reading	Ending Odometer Reading	Total Miles Traveled	Expenses Incurred (gas, tolls, etc.)

Destination:		Primary Purpose of Trip:	

Date	Starting Odometer Reading	Ending Odometer Reading	Total Miles Traveled	Expenses Incurred (gas, tolls, etc.)

Destination:		Primary Purpose of Trip:	

BUSINESS: 50¢/mi   CHARITY: 14¢/mi   MED: 16.5¢/mi   MOVE: 16.5¢/mi

This Vehicle Log is NOT copyrighted. Feel free to duplicate it for your own use.

You Get $500.00 in Tax Deductions for Every 1,000 Business Miles You Drive!

Not taking this deduction is like throwing a $1.00 bill out your window every time you put two business miles on your car! Or think of it this way: You could be getting **some $200.00 in tax deductions for every tank of gas** you put in your car. (Maybe that will make it a little easier to deal with the outrageous price of gas these days!)

If you put 10,000 business miles on your car in 2010, with simple recordkeeping you can qualify for **$5,000 in *new* tax deductions**.

What About Errands and Shopping?

What about shopping trips and other errands? Often there are ways those miles could become tax-deductible also. Let's look at a few examples...

Do you need to go to a shopping mall to purchase a birthday present for your sister? With a few seconds of advance planning, this one is easy, because you have so many options to use. For example, if there is a quick-copy center in the mall, and you need to have copies of your business flyers printed, you could go to the mall to have your flyers printed. While you're there, get your sister's gift.

This mileage would be deductible if <u>Business</u> was your <u>Primary</u> purpose, and <u>shopping</u> was a <u>secondary</u> purpose of your trip. The *secondary* purpose is *not* recorded in your vehicle-use log. If there are two purposes for a specific trip, which one is Primary? **Federal Tax Courts** have said the taxpayer (you) makes that determination.

In the above example, you could substitute any reasonable and necessary business purpose in place of the "quick-copy center" example – such as, buying office supplies, customer prospecting, etc.

Going to the mall for personal reasons only, produces Zero-percent tax deduction. Going to the mall for a business reason, produces 100-percent tax deduction. Add the two separate trips, and only 50% of your total mileage is deductible.

But combining the errands into one trip produces a 100% deduction.

So, each time you are about to run a **business errand**, pause for a second and ask yourself if there a **personal errand** you need to run that you could do at the same time and in the same location?

And, each time you are about to run a **personal errand**, pause for a second and ask yourself if there a **business errand** you need to run that you could do at the same time and in the same location?

Sometimes the answer will be 'no.' But you'd be surprised at how often the answer turns out to be 'yes.'

How Do You Figure the Amount of
Tax Deductions for Business Use of Your Vehicle?

You have Two Options.

The IRS gives you the option of determining the value of your vehicle-use deductions by using the "Standard Mileage Rate" (SMR) method or the "Actual Operating Cost" method.   **[IRS Proc. 94-73]**

The **STANDARD MILEAGE RATE** (SMR) method involves simply using the vehicle-use log to determine your total Business miles, and then multiply that number by the Standard Mileage Rate (50¢/mile for 2010).

The Standard Mileage Rate is determined by the IRS annually, and tends to change almost every year. For 2010, the rate is 50 cents per mile. So if you put 10,000 business miles on your car in 2010, you will have $5,000 in vehicle deductions, using the SMR method.

The "**ACTUAL OPERATING COST METHOD**" option requires keeping a record of vehicle operating costs for the full year.   This option requires more recordkeeping, but may give you a substantially higher deduction in many circumstances.

If you choose Option 2, which is based on your
<u>Actual Vehicle Operating Costs</u>:

From your 90-day Vehicle Use Log records, determine what ***percentage*** of your <u>total</u> miles were driven for Business purposes, to determine the "*business use percentage*" of your vehicle.

1. Add-up your total vehicle operating costs for the entire year (actually it's very easy – I'll show you how a couple of pages later), and then multiply that dollar amount by your Business Use Percentage. The resulting figure will be the amount you can deduct on your Tax Return for tax-deductible Vehicle Operating Costs.

In addition, when you use the Actual Operating Cost method you can ***also*** claim an amount for depreciation (let your Tax Pro do this).

For example, if you drove your car 14,000 miles during the year, and 10,000 of those were "business miles," your business use percentage (BUP) would be 71%. So you would multiply your total actual vehicle operating costs by 0.71, and you will have determined the amount of tax write-off you can claim using the Actual Operating Cost Method (plus depreciation, remember).

The "actual cost" option may give you higher deduction:

- when gas prices are high
- if you have a 'gas guzzler'

- if you have frequent or expensive repairs and maintenance,
- if you drive an exceptionally expensive car.

What, exactly, are "Vehicle Operating Costs?" That term applies to just about any expense that you have because you <u>have</u> a vehicle, that you would <u>not</u> have it you did <u>not</u> have a vehicle. If you did not operate a vehicle you would not need car insurance, would not pay for car washes, and wouldn't pay license and registration fees. So those are example of Actual Vehicle Operating Costs."

Here are more examples...

- **Depreciation**
- Lease Payments
- **Gasoline**
- Oil and oil changes
- **Front end alignments**
- Wheel balancing
- **New tires**
- Tune ups
- **Repairs**
- Maintenance
- **Windshield wipers**
- Car washes, waxes and detailing
- **New battery**
- License & Registration fees

- **Automobile Insurance**

- Depreciation

- **Collision deductibles**

- Road Hazard Insurance (such as AAA)

- **Extended warrantees**

- Repairs

- **Road Emergency supplies (flares, road hazard signs, etc)**

- Garage Rent

- etc., etc., etc.

[IRS Pub 463]

Does that sound like a lot to keep track of? It doesn't need to be a chore. Keeping track of your actual vehicle operating costs does not have to result in a shoebox full of receipts.

Here is a three-part process that ***dramatically reduces your paperwork*** burden:

Part One:

Take a credit card with a zero balance – a card that you would not have to use for anything else, and begin using it to pay for all vehicle operating cost whenever possible.

Part Two:

Some costs, such as car payments, cannot be paid with a credit card, so for those, write checks.

Take a sheet of lined paper and draw 4 vertical lines to make 5 columns. Label it "Vehicle Costs Paid by Check," and whenever you pay a vehicle expense by check, record:

> Date written
>
> Check Number
>
> Payee
>
> Amount of check
>
> Purpose/Expense

Whenever you fill up a page, add up the subtotal for that page, put it in your tax file, and start a new sheet.

Part Three:

There will always be some car-related expenses you pay for with cash – street-side parking meters, tolls, windshield washer fluid, etc. These small expenses can add up to a lot of missed deductions if you don't have a way to record the cash expenditures. Suggestion: Get a small (2" x 3") spiral notebook, insert a short golf pencil in the spiral of the notebook, and put it in your console or glove compartment because you will probably be in your car when these cash expenses come up.

At the end of the year you:

Step 1. Add up the totals from your 12 monthly credit card statements.

Step 2. Add up the totals from your list of vehicle-related check payments.

Step 3. Add up cash expenses from your notebook.

Step 4. Combine those 3 numbers, and you have total vehicle costs for the year.

Still sound too difficult? Try one of these two options:

If you use the quick and efficient software program named the **Home Business Tax Records *Made Easy!*™** or the world's easiest "pencil and paper" recordkeeping system **Tax MiniMi$er™**, ALL of your record-keeping chores will become easy, including the costs of operating your vehicle. **You can download a free 30-day trial version** of the Home Business Tax Records *Made Easy!*, or purchase the software or the MiniMi$er very inexpensively at **www.HomeBusinessTaxSavings.com**

Which Method Is Available to YOU, and which is Best for YOU?

The SMR method may be used whether you own or lease your vehicle.

If you **OWN** your vehicle and want to use the SMR, you must choose it in the first year the vehicle is available for business use; in later years you may choose either method.

IMPORTANT NOTE: If you used the Section 179 Election when you purchased your vehicle, you are not eligible to use the SMR.

If you **<u>LEASE</u>** your vehicle and wish to use the SMR method, you must use it for the entire lease (including renewals). **[IRS Pub. 583]**

Regardless of whether you use the Standard Mileage Rate method or the Actual Cost method, you can <u>also</u> deduct 100% of **parking** fees and **tolls** incurred while driving for business purposes.

[IRS Proc. 90-59, and IRS Bulletin 1990-52 § 4.04]

And, regardless of which method you select, you can <u>also</u> deduct the business-use percentage of the **interest** paid on your vehicle loan, and the business use percentage of your **Personal Property Taxes**.

[IRS Proc. 95-54 § 5.04]

What if you are leasing your vehicle? You can deduct the business use percentage of your lease payments, plus the business use percentage of your vehicle operating costs, adjusted for depreciation. (Trust me, have your tax pro calculate this for you.)

IMPORTANT NOTES:

(1) You can usually shift between the Standard Mileage Rate and the Actual Cost Method at any time, so it is best to keep both types of records and select the one that gives you the best deductions at year-end.

(2) You cannot use the Standard Mileage Rate method if you have claimed a Section 179 deduction for that same vehicle.

(3) BUP of interest on a car loan is deductible if you are self-employed.

(4) Parking and tolls for business use are deductible in addition to either method. **[IRC § 168 and Revenue Procedure 2008-72]**

Some "Non-Business" Miles *Also* Can be Deducted if You Itemize Your Tax Deductions

You can also deduct miles spent doing charitable work, miles going to and from medical appointments, and miles for moving/relocating to a new job location (if it is at least 50 miles away).

These rates also tend to change frequently, but for year 2010 the mileage deduction allowances are set as follows:

> **Business Mileage** = **50.0¢/mile**
>
> **Charitable Work** = **14.0¢/mile**
>
> **Medical Care** = **16.5¢/mile**
>
> **Moving/Relocating** = **16.5¢/mile**

What About Depreciation?

Claiming depreciation on the car or truck you use for business purposes gives you additional tax advantages.

If you use the "Actual Cost Method" and your vehicle is considered "Listed Property," and the depreciation "recovery period" is generally five years.

Beware, however, if the business use percentage of your vehicle falls _below 50 percent_ before the end of the 5-year "recovery period," special depreciation rules apply (and they are not in your favor).

[IRS Publication 946, Section 280F]

If this happens, you must re-compute the depreciation using the straight-line method **[IRC § 280F(b)(2)(B)]** and any excess depreciation then becomes taxable income.   **[IRC § 280F(b)(1) and 168(g)]**

If you use the Standard Mileage Rate method, depreciation is "built into" the SMR rate, so you are not affected by the 50% rule just discussed.

What are the Tax Implications When You Sell or Trade-in Your Vehicle?

First of all, you should seriously consider the potential tax impact, when deciding whether to trade-in your vehicle or to sell it on your own.

When you sell a vehicle on your own, you'll usually get more money for your car, than if you trade-in the vehicle. From a tax standpoint, when you sell the vehicle you will report either a gain or a loss on your tax return for the business portion of the vehicle you sell.

If your decision is to trade-in the vehicle towards the cost of purchasing another one, any gain or loss will be transferred into the "basis" ("cost," for tax purposes) of the new vehicle. In the case of a 'gain,' you will defer the gain into the new vehicle by adjusting the basis downward.

To determine whether you will have a gain or loss on the sale of your business vehicle (for tax purposes), you will need to compute the accumulated depreciation that has been taken over the business life of the vehicle. This accumulated depreciation lowers the "basis" or "net tax value" on the company records.

For Example...

Bill bought a car for $20,000 on January 1, 2007, and used it 60% for business. The "starting basis" (or "depreciable basis") of the vehicle is $12,000 (60% of $20,000). For simplicity sake, let us assume that the depreciation allowed for 2007, 2008, and 2009 was $2,000 per year. As of 12/31/09 (three years after purchase of the vehicle), the tax basis of the vehicle had been reduced to $6,000 ($12,000 starting basis, minus the $6,000 accumulated depreciation).

If Bill sold his car on 12/31/09 for $8,000, he would have incurred a business loss calculated as follows:

Since the car was used 60% for business, the business portion of the sales price was $4,800 (60% of $8,000). Since the business basis was $6,000, Bill had a deductible business loss of $1,200.

In addition, Bill had a loss on the personal-use portion of the vehicle. However, this loss is *not* tax deductible.

Let's take a look at another scenario...

It is possible that Bill may have been able to trade-in this same vehicle for $12,000 towards the purchase price of a new vehicle.

In this case, Bill would have had a "gain" (profit) on the disposition of the old vehicle, and that gain would be deferred into the new vehicle by adjusting the basis of the new vehicle. (In English, that means if his 'profit' was $2,000 and he bought an $18,000 car, we would pretend he paid $20,000 for the new car, for purposes of calculating depreciation on the new vehicle.)

Since the gain was "carried forward" into the new vehicle, no gain or loss would be reported on Bill's tax return.

If this seems confusing, that's because it **IS** confusing. (Hey, my eyes are glazing over just *writing* this stuff!) **Recommendation: Don't even try – get your tax pro to help.**

For taxpayers who take the option to calculate vehicle deductions on their tax return by using the Standard Mileage Rate method, there is a built-in amount for depreciation that must be factored-in to determine if there is a gain or loss on the disposition of the vehicle.

No matter how old your car is, or how many miles you've put on it, a vehicle cannot be depreciated below zero. If your depreciation gets down to zero, your SMR continues as before, but with <u>none</u> of the deduction allocated to depreciation.   **[IRS Proc. 98-63]**

Also consider the "Section 179 Elections" we discussed earlier. The "accelerated depreciation" under §179 applies also to the purchase of business-use vehicles, although there are special limits on depreciation you can take in the first year. Congress may also reinstate "Bonus Depreciation" incentives, which expired at the end of 2008.

> For CURRENT INFORMATION on Section 179 Elections and other Tax Incentives for Vehicle Buyers, download the Special Report **"Tax Breaks for Vehicle Buyers"** at **www.HomeBusinessTaxSavings.com** under **"Resource Center"**

Here's How to Increase Your Vehicle Deductions by an *ADDITIONAL 50%!*

The following is a valuable tax strategy if your family has two vehicles, each worth approximately the same value, and if at least two-thirds of the total miles driven (on both cars combined, not individually) qualify as business miles.

For example: Let's say you put 35,000 miles on your car, and 30,000 of those miles qualify as "business miles." And let's say your spouse drives 5,000 miles, but none are tax-deductible business miles. And let's say each car is worth about $20,000. That means

- Your total "family miles" equals 40,000 miles.

- 30,000 of those 40,000 miles (75%) are business miles.

If you put all those business miles on one car, you will be limited to the expenses and depreciation limits on one vehicle. The other car will receive no tax deductions, because no miles qualify as business.

However, if you alternate use of the two vehicles, you will still drive 30,000 business miles, but you will put 15,000 of those miles on each of the two cars. Your spouse still drives 5,000 personal miles, but he/she puts 2,500 of those miles on each of the two vehicles.

You may now claim 75% of the miles put on each of the two vehicles, and your vehicle use and depreciation tax-deduction limit increases to $30,000, instead of being capped at under $20,000. **This could result in a 50% increase in your vehicle deductions!**

Always consult with a professional Tax Advisor before buying, leasing, selling or trading a vehicle you will use in your business. Failure to do so could be _very_ costly!

It's easy to keep IRS-compliant records "on-the-fly' with the Tax MiniMi$er, which transforms your ordinary Day Planner into a bullet-proof Daily Tax Diary. The Tax MiniMi$er is a written accounting method which compliments any computerized tax recordkeeping system such as the Home Business Tax Savings *Made Easy!* software. Review them both by visiting www.HomeBusinessTaxSavings.com

You May *Never* Take Another *Vacation.* From now on, ALL of your Travel could become Tax-Deductible Business Trips!!

A business based in your home may have broad 'territorial limits.' Your customers, clients or prospects may be anywhere in the United States, or North America, or even the world, depending on your business.

This means that, wherever you travel **you <u>could</u> be traveling on business**, and reasonable business-travel expenses are tax-deductible, even if combined with personal travel or family vacations! The IRS rules about tax-deductibility of business travel are <u>very specific</u>, but they are also very easy to comply with, so you should have no problem making sure you are staying within the legal parameters.

The tax code says that anytime your work "requires you to sleep or rest away from your principle place of business" (that may be your home), you may deduct reasonable travel and related expenses (such as meals, hotel, rental car, tips, etc.).**[IRC Section § 162(a)(2) and Revenue Rulings 54-497, 75-432, 63-145, 75-169, 76-453]**

The IRS's 3-Part Test

Be sure that the <u>Primary</u> purpose of the travel is <u>Business</u> (more on that later) and pass the IRS's "3-Part Test":

ANOTHER MYTH TO DISPEL: A trip does NOT become 'Business Travel' just because "everyone is a prospect." For a trip to qualify, it must meet ALL of the requirements described in this chapter.

1. The travel must be **usual and customary** within your type of business.

2. The travel must be conducted with the **intent** to obtain a **direct business benefit.**

3. The travel must be appropriate and helpful to **developing and maintaining** your business.

You Also Must Meet the "51/49% Transportation Rule"

For travel within the U.S., when you combine business travel with personal travel, the tax code allows you to deduct 100% of your transportation costs, in addition to lodging and meal deductions…

- If the *Primary* purpose of your trip is *Business*, and
- If more than ½ of your days away qualify as "Business days."

[IRC Section § 1.162-2(b)(2)]

What is Considered a "Business Day?"

'Business Days' generally include (a) **travel days** getting to and from your business destination, (b) days on which you spend more than **four hours on business** related activities, and (c) any day on which you attend a **pre-scheduled business appointment**.

If the primary purpose of your travel is business, the cost of round trip transportation to your "business destination" is tax deductible, whether you travel First Class air, Coach Class, train, car, boat or even on a privately chartered plane (if justifiable under the circumstances). Note: For a transportation day to qualify as a Business day, it must take you at least four hours to get from the door of your home to the door of your hotel.

[IRS Regulations, § 1.274-4(d)(2)(i)]

Once you arrive at your destination, you will incur certain other expenses, such as taxi fares or car rental, hotel, meals, tips, etc. Most of these are 100% deductible, except for meals, which are only 50% deductible, and only on the "business days," not personal days.

You may deduct food and lodging expenses for "Business Days" even if your trip does not include enough business days for it to qualify as a "Business Trip." For example, if you make a five day trip, but only two days are spent on business, you may deduct your meals and hotel for those two days only, but you may not claim any of the transportation costs, because the trip will not have met the 51/49% Transportation Rule discussed earlier.

What is a Pre-Scheduled Business Appointment?

Pre-scheduled means arrangements were made before you began your trip. *Business Appointment* means any meeting or activity that would customarily be considered "business" in your industry or business category.

On a day you attend a pre-scheduled business appointment, the <u>full day</u> is considered a Business Day, regardless of how much (*or how little!*) time is involved.   In order to qualify, you must (1) schedule it **<u>in advance</u>**, (2) **<u>attend</u>** the appointment or activity, and (3) **<u>prove</u>** that you attended the appointment. Example…

SETTING IT UP:

Let's say you want to combine a family vacation to Disneyland, with a business trip to the Los Angeles area. Who do you know in the LA area who is in the same type of business as you are, and is more successful than you? (This is easy if you are in network marketing.) Call or email that person and ask if he or she would be willing to meet you for breakfast one morning while you are in town. They'll probably agree to meet with you, and even agree to meet at your own hotel.

To **<u>prove</u> you have a pre-scheduled business appointment**, for tax purposes, write an email thanking the person for agreeing to meet with you at (insert date, time, place) because you are very interested to talk/learn about (fill in specific business purpose).

Print out a copy of the email, and put it in your tax file as proof the meeting was pre-scheduled.

PROVING YOU ATTENDED THE APPOINTMENT:

Proving it was pre-scheduled is only half of the "proof" the IRS will want to see. The other half is proof that you actually <u>attended</u> the appointment. How do you do that?

Option 1: If you met a person for breakfast, you probably picked up the tab. In order to write-off the expense as Business Entertainment (see next chapter), you will record information that proves you met for breakfast. Option 2: When you return home (or before) send an email to that same person, thanking them for meeting with you, and mentioning some specific business benefit you got from the meeting. Print out that email, attach it to the one you sent before the trip, and, together, those two emails will prove it was prescheduled, and attended.

What About Weekends and Holidays?

If weekend days and/or holidays fall between Business Days, they are considered by the IRS to be Business Days. For example, if you travel to a destination on Wednesday, do business on Thursday and Friday, and your next pre-scheduled appointment is on the following Monday, Saturday and

Sunday <u>could</u> be considered Business Days, as well as Friday and Monday. AND if Monday 'happens' to be a government holiday, your next business day could be on Tuesday, and the 3-day weekend gives you three additional business days.

The test is this: Would it be practical to return home for the weekend days? If so, they are not deductible. But if it would not be practical to return home (due to the expense or the time required), they will be considered to be Business Days, regardless of what you actually do on those days.

[Reg § 1.274-4(d)(2)(v)]

What About Saturday-Night Stay-Overs?

Oftentimes airlines offer substantial fare discounts if a Saturday night stay is included.   **Good news for you!**   If a substantial discount is available by including a Saturday night stay, Saturday may be considered a (tax-deductible) "Business *Stay-over* Day" and Sunday is considered a (tax-deductible) "Business *Travel* Day." In order to qualify, you must be able to show that the amount of money saved on air fare is greater than the additional costs of staying over.   **[PLR 9237014]**

Exactly, What Can I Deduct?

If your trip qualifies as Business Travel, you may deduct 100% of your round-trip transportation expenses, 100% of your lodging costs, taxis, rental cars, tips and incidentals, plus 50% of your meals on "business days."

When you are required to remain out-of-town for one or more nights for business, you can also deduct the cost of laundering or dry cleaning any clothing soiled on that trip, even if you wait and have the cleaning done upon your return home.

Personal grooming expenses (haircuts, manicures) incurred just prior to a business trip, are NOT deductible, BUT if you wait and incur those expenses while you are ON the trip, they ARE deductible.

[Internal Revenue Ruling 63-145 and 1963-2 C.B. 86]

Lesson: Maybe we should plan our business trips when our clothes are dirty and we need a haircut. Not a recommendation, just a thought.

What is 'Per Diem' and Why Should You Care?

When government employees travel on government business, they are paid a "Per Diem" (per day) rate, which covers their Lodging, Meals and Incidental Expenses.

You can find current Per Diem rates online at www.gsa.gov/perdiem .

Business travelers who are not government employees or military, may **not** use Per Diem for **Lodging**; however, if you are a sole-proprietor, a partnership, or an LLC filing as sole-proprietor status, you **DO** have the option of deducting the government Per Diem rate for Meals & Incidental Expenses (M&IE). **[IRC §162(a)(2)]**

Why would you want to do that? Two reasons: (a) you have NO recordkeeping requirements whatsoever, and (b) the amount you can claim depends solely upon the established rate for the location you are visiting, and how many days you will be there. If you're the kind of person who books hotel rooms that have kitchenettes, visit a grocery store upon arrival, and prepare your own meals, you could actually come out way ahead, because the established Per Diem rate may be much higher than the amount you actually spend on food and incidentals. What are Incidentals? Examples include fees and tips to porters, baggage carriers, bellhops, maids.

Good news – you do not have to decide prior to the trip. Keep track of your actual expenses while you are on your trip. When you get back home, compare your actual expenses with the Per Diem amounts, and use whichever is better for you.

For partial days, a rule of thumb is 15% of the M&IE rate for Breakfast, 30% for Lunch, 50% for Dinner and 5% for Incidentals.

CAVEAT: Per Diem cannot be used for an employee who owns more than 10% of the company. This does not apply to sole proprietors, because there is no "company."

What about partial days, such as arrival days and departure days. Here's the table for determining the amount you may claim on those days.

The M&IE rates differ by travel location. View the per diem rate at www.gsa.gov/mie to determine which M&IE rates apply for your primary destination.   2010 FEDERAL PER DIEM RATES

M&IE Total	$46	$51	$56	$61	$66	$71
Breakfast	7	8	9	10	11	12
Lunch	11	12	13	15	16	18
Dinner	23	26	29	31	34	36
Incidentals	5	5	5	5	5	5

Does It Make Any Difference
What <u>Method</u> of Transportation I Use?

Simple answer: Not really. If you travel by car, truck, plane, train, boat or motorcycle, your actual travel expenses are 100% fully deductible if the trip qualifies as "business travel." Deductibility also is independent of "class" of transportation. You could travel First Class or even by chartered aircraft or limousine, *as long as the expense would not be considered "lavish" or "extravagant" considering the specific facts and circumstances.*

[IRS Publication 463]

Can I Claim My Spouse's Expenses if He or She Accompanies Me to a Business Meeting or Convention?

Expenses of an accompanying spouse could possibly be deductible, but **only if**:

- Their travel is for a bona fide business purpose (i.e., not just accompanying you),

- He or she is an employee or owner of the business (see Chapter Seven for details), or

- The travel and related expenses would be deductible for him/her even if he/she were making the trip alone.

[IRC Section § 274(m)(3)]

An auditor would approach it this way: Would you have paid (as a business expense) for this employee to join you on this business trip *even if you were not related to him or her?* Of course, your answer has to be "yes."

What About Seminars on Cruise Ships?

About those "seminars" held on cruise ships ... well...   They're not exactly deductible. (Sorry.)

Expenses for "business meetings" or "professional seminars" held on ***any Foreign Flag Carrier*** ship (which is essentially ALL cruise ships), ***is not deductible***. Period.

So, how CAN you take a tax-deductible cruise? At least two ways…

First. If your business involves booking cruise travel, just about any travel on a cruise ship could be a "familiarization trip" (Fam Trip, in industry jargon).

Second. Instead of having your seminar or business meeting ON the ship, what if it took place <u>ashore</u>, at the furthest point from your Port of Departure?

Then, your cruise ship becomes a ***means of transportation***, which you could elect to use in lieu of air travel. Remember a few pages ago we established that the ***means*** of transportation ***or class of service***, had no effect on the deductibility of business trip transportation!

One way to get to a seminar location in the Caribbean would be to fly, but another option might be to travel by cruise ship, right? The IRS calls this "luxury water transportation." If that ship happens to make a few stops at other ports-of-call on the way to, or on the way back from, the seminar port … oh well!

> **NOTE: You will have to be able to prove the legitimacy of the meeting, and to justify the meeting location being**

outside of continental United States, but those aren't high hurdles.

But How Much Can I Deduct?

As we have just learned, on business travel, you can normally deduct 100% of your transportation, 100% of your lodging, 50% of your meals, and 100% of your incidental expenses.

But on a cruise, all of those expenses are usually combined into an "all inclusive" fare.

Good news! Easy answer! (Can you believe it? A tax question with an easy answer?)

When you travel via cruise ship *as a means of transportation* you may deduct 200% of the maximum Per Diem rate authorized anywhere in the continental United States at that same time of year.

For example, if the highest Per Diem rate in continental U.S. is $400.00 -- **including lodging**, as well as meals and incidentals – so, you could deduct up to $800 per day ($400 x 2) for using a cruise ship as a means of transportation to a business meeting or professional seminar.

Let's Summarize the Deductions for Business Travel

"Ordinary and Necessary" business expenses include:

- 50% of the cost of all meals on Business Days

  [Reg § 1.162-2(a)]

- 100% of transportation and lodging costs

  [IRS Publication 463]

- 100% of laundry and dry cleaning of clothing soiled during business portion of trip   **[Internal Revenue Ruling 63-145 and 1963-2 C.B. 86]**

- Business-related telephone calls, both local and long distance

  [Reg § 1.162-2(a)]

- Local transportation from airport to hotel, to customer meetings, and back to airport (including taxis, limos, trains, buses, rental cars, etc.)

  [IRS Publication 463]

- All appropriate tips and gratuities associated with otherwise-deductible expenses   **[IRS Publication 463]**

The Rules for Keeping Bullet-Proof Business-Trip Records are EASY, but STRICT!

This is not difficult unless you procrastinate. All the IRS requires is the answers to 5 questions:

1. *What* Was the Money Spent On?

List each individual expenditure, such as plane tickets, taxi fares, meals (listed separately), tips, registration fees, etc.

2. *When* Did You Spend It?

Dates and times of departure and return, as well as date of each expenditure.

3. *Where* Did You Spend It?

City you flew to, restaurant where you dined, from-and-to of each taxi fare, name of hotel you stayed in, who you gave tips to (bellman, taxi driver, maid), etc.

4. *Why* Did You Spend It?

Justify the business purpose of the trip itself, and the business reason for each expenditure. Not everything is 'automatically' deductible. For example, in-room hotel movie rentals and purchases from a hotel room mini-bar are normally not deductible.

5. *Can You Prove* You Paid Your Bills?

You'll need copies of paid receipts for hotel stays, transportation expenses (other than local transportation such as taxi), conference fees, and any individual expenditures over $75.

What… When … Where …Why … Prove You Spent It.

And this documentation **MUST be made within 24 hours** of when you spent the money. <u>The IRS can be very STRICT about this</u>.

Here's How to Turn this 'Chore' Into a Simple 'Habit'

1. Carry a small spiral-bound notebook in your pocket with a golf pencil tucked in the spiral, and a paper-clip on the back cover, or use the professional *Tax MiniMi$er*™ recordkeeping system, which you can obtain at www.HomeBusinessTaxSavings.com .

2. Every time you spend a penny on anything (even non-deductible expenses), record it in your *Tax MiniMi$er* and save it in the built-in receipt envelope, or record it in your notebook and clip the receipt inside the back cover.

3. Each evening, review your *Tax MiniMi$er* or notebook to make sure everything you wrote is clearly legible, and write notes on your receipts to remind you (if you are audited three years later) what each receipt was for.

4. Put that day's receipts in the built-in receipt pocket in your *Tax MiniMi$er*, or staple them together and put them in a safe place, like your suitcase or briefcase.

Then, immediately upon return to your home or office enter the data into your tax deduction tracking software and file the receipts with your tax records.

NOTE: There are special rules for deducting business travel expenses for trips outside the United States and the North American Area. Download **"Rules for Deducting International Business Travel"** at no cost, from the 'Resource Center' at www.HomeBusinessTaxSavings.com

---

CHAPTER TEN

Meals and Entertainment Expenses Legally May be Deductible, Too!

The IRS lumps together the broad categories of Entertainment, Business Meals, Business-Related Sports, Recreation and Amusement under the tax heading "Entertainment."

First, in order to be deductible a meal or an entertainment expense must be "ordinary and necessary" to carrying on your type of business. *Ordinary and Necessary* is usually interpreted to mean usual and helpful.

[IRC §274 and §162]

Be Aware of the 50% Rule!

There is one significant difference between tax-deductible meals and entertainment expenses and nearly all other tax-deductible business expenses: Since 1994, qualifying **meal & entertainment** expenses generally are **deductible at only 50% of their actual cost**, although there are a few exceptions that allow for 100% deduction (such as employee picnics and business entertainment in your home). **[IRC§274(n)]**

Here's How to Determine Whether Entertainment IS or is NOT Legally Deductible...

There are only three terms you must be familiar with:

1. **Four-Requirement Test**
2. **Clear Business Setting**
3. **Associated Entertainment**

1. "The Four-Requirement Test"

If you meet <u>all four steps</u> of the **Four-Requirement Test** you probably have a qualifying business entertainment expense.

The Four Requirements are:

1. At the time you decided to spend the money, you expected that there would be a <u>future business benefit</u> from the meeting.

2. During the entertainment, you specifically <u>talked about</u> things that could produce that business benefit.

3. Your <u>principal reason</u> for entertaining this person was to actively conduct business.

4. You incurred the expense so that you could <u>talk directly with the person</u> who could produce the future business benefit.

It is also helpful if you can show that the person you are entertaining knows that you are spending money on him/her in order to directly attempt to further your business interests, and that you have no meaningful social or personal relationship with the person or people you are entertaining.

2. "Clear Business Setting"

In addition, your entertainment must take place in a **Clear Business Setting**.

Generally, that means an environment relatively free from distractions that would interfere with the business discussion. Restaurants, your own home, hotel meeting rooms and hotel dining rooms, for example, are considered to be "conducive to business discussion without significant distraction."

Thus, business entertainment taking place in these locations are deemed to be in a "Clear Business Setting."

Locations ***not*** considered to be "clear business setting," include night clubs, theaters, sporting events, and stage shows, because these locations all have distractions that make it unlikely that a serious business discussion would or could take place. However, entertainment in these locations **<u>may very well</u> qualify for deduction under the "Associated Entertainment" Rule...**

3. "Associated Entertainment"

"Associated Entertainment" is entertainment that is <u>not directly</u> for the purpose of conducting business discussions, but is <u>indirectly associated</u> with conduct of business.   **[Rev Reg §1.274-2(a) and (d)(3)]**

Entertainment that takes place **during the same calendar day** as a meeting or entertainment in a clear business setting, may be considered "Associated Entertainment."

Note: This is a newly revised definition. Until recently, to qualify as Associated Entertainment, an activity needed to take place immediately before or immediately following active "conduct of business." The new definition is much more liberal.   **[IRC §274(d)]**

Let's look at some examples.

Let's say you take prospective clients to the theater and then after the event, you take them to dinner and have (to use IRS terminology) a "substantial and bona fide business discussion." The dinner expense falls under Clear Business Setting and the theater expense falls under Associated Entertainment, so both would be deductible at 50% of their actual cost.

Or, let's say you call a business prospect or client to arrange a dinner meeting for <u>tomorrow night</u>, and while on the phone, say "how about some tennis <u>tomorrow morning</u>?"

The tennis would be deductible as "Associated Entertainment" and the dinner as an "Entertainment" expense, since the Associated Entertainment took place during the same calendar day as the business discussion.

Sometimes You Can Deduct *Your Own* Meal Expense Even If You Do <u>Not</u> Pay for <u>Theirs</u>

Yes, under two circumstances. The first is when you are on an overnight business trip (at the 50% rate, of course). But there's another one that most people do not know about…

If you go to lunch with some folks you work with at your office, and you position yourself to sit next to a particular person you want to have a business discussion with, even if you each pay for your own meal, you may be eligible to deduct your own meal under the "Dutch Treat Rule." The amount you can deduct is 50% **<u>minus</u> the amount "you *would have spent* if you had eaten at home**."

Here's how you determine amount you would have spent if you had eaten at home…

1. You go shopping for one week's groceries for your family.

2. Do not buy any items that are not food.

3. Add up all the food costs.

4. Divide by the number of people in your household.

5. Divide that number by 7, and the result will be the average amount you spend <u>per day</u> on <u>meals for one person</u> at home.

Not all meals cost the same, so use a logical allocation of the costs, such as 20% of the daily food cost for your breakfast, 30% for lunch and 50% for your dinner.

For example: If your daily food cost average is $5.00, then $1.00 is assumed to be for breakfast, $1.50 for lunch and $2.50 for dinner.

So, to apply the "Dutch Treat Rule," you'd take 50% of the amount of your lunch receipt, and then subtract $1.50 – the amount you would have spent if you had eaten lunch at home. The resultant figure is the amount you can deduct under the Meals and Entertainment category on your Schedule C. If your meal cost $18.00, for example, 50% would be $9.00. Subtract $1.50, and the amount you could write-off would be $7.50. Doesn't sound like much?

This deduction could be worth <u>thousands</u> if you **often** have breakfast, lunch and/or dinner with prospective customers or associates to discuss business, but don't pick up their tab. If your Dutch Treat deductions average $20 per week, for example, your deductions from this category alone would be more than $1,000!

Regarding documentation, even if you are claiming only your own meal expenses, you will still be required to record, on your receipt or in your day planner, the same five items specified in the next section in this chapter. For individual meal or entertainment expenses under $75 each, you do not need a receipt, but you still need to answer the five questions in your documentation. A notation in your daily planner is usually sufficient.

Even GOLF *Might* be Deductible
(as may some other leisure activities)

Are you a golfer? Want to deduct greens fees and/or lunch in the grill? Golf is one participation sport that can probably qualify under the Four Requirements Rule, and definitely qualify under the Associated Entertainment Rule. Of course you cannot play golf with the same people every week and still qualify, but if you're the type of person who likes to take prospects to the club with you, this is ideal.

Unlike most other sports, golf offers ample opportunity to "hold substantial business discussions" while walking or riding down the fairway, while waiting on the tee for the foursome ahead to putt-out, or while waiting for a fellow player across the fairway to hit his or her shot. You may be able to claim that the golf course was a location "conducive to business discussion without significant distraction."

But to make <u>absolutely sure</u> that your deduction is allowed, simply host your guests to lunch in the club dining room or grill before or following your round of golf. Claim the meal expense under "Clear Business Setting," and claim the golf as "Associated Entertainment."

Other activities that might be treated similarly, depending on the circumstances, include boating and fishing. And you can probably think of others as well. In each case, be sure that you meet The Four-Requirement Test as explained above, or claim it as Associated Entertainment if you had a bona fide business discussion during the same 24-hour day.

Documenting Business-Entertainment Expenses is Not Difficult, but the Rules Are STRICT!

The simplest way to document your tax-deductible entertainment expenses is to get a receipt for everything, staple related receipts together, and write, in ink, directly on the receipt (**within 24 hours**!) the following:

- **The <u>Date</u> the expense was incurred.**
  Generally this means the date of the entertainment itself (i.e., if you purchased season tickets to a sporting event to entertain clients and prospects, you would record the date, etc., of each individual event, as it occurred).

  [Reg Sec 1.274-5(b)(3)(ii)]

- **The <u>Amount</u> of the expense.**
  The numbers imprinted on the front of the receipt can fade over time, becoming illegible, so write the amount on the receipt in ink.

  [Reg Sec 1.274-2(b)(1)(i) and Reg. 1.274-5T(c)(2)(iii)(B)]

- **The <u>Place</u> the expense was incurred.**
  Name and location of the venue, as well as the type of event, if not obvious. List the place of the bona fide business discussion also, if the deduction was "Associated Entertainment."

  [Reg Sec 1.274-5(b)(3)(iii)]

- **Your <u>Purpose</u> for incurring the expense.**
  Be sure to relate your "why" to your business, of course. Why are you entertaining this particular person, and what business result do you expect to come about as a result?

  [Reg Sec 1.274-5(b)(3)(iv)]

- **The <u>Relationship</u> to you of the person(s) you entertained**
  or job title, and other relevant information that explains why you entertained that particular person.

  [Reg Sec 1.274-5(b)(3)(v)]

READ THIS!

This *documentation* MUST be recorded <u>within 24 hours</u> of incurring the entertainment expense, so it is a good habit to do this as soon as you return to your home, office or hotel that night. I recommend you input this information into your *Home Business Tax Records Made Easy!* software or your *Tax MiniMi$er* recordkeeping system, and then file the paper receipts in your tax file, as additional back-up.

Want a Professional Recommendation?

Keep really good records. This area is frequently looked at in audits, but <u>that's only because</u> most people don't know the rules and record-keeping requirements, so it's easy to "catch" taxpayers who don't have proper records.

But if you follow these two steps for all of your Meal and Entertainment deductions, the documentation will be audit-proof:

1. Answer, <u>in writing</u>, <u>all five</u> documentation questions for <u>each</u> deductible expense, and

2. <u>Record</u> those answers <u>within 24 hours</u> of the time the expense was incurred.

If your own circumstances are such that you could derive large tax savings in this category, be sure to obtain good tax advice from someone highly experienced in home-business tax law. Oftentimes making just a minor adjustment ***in advance*** can turn a non-deductible expense into a deductible one.

> **Want some help remembering what facts to write down, in order to have IRS-compliant documentation for Meals & Entertainment expenses? Make a page of peel-off stickers with those 5 topics pre-written on them.**

CHAPTER ELEVEN

Don't Dread that Dreaded Word, *"Documentation"*

We learned in Chapter Eight how quick and easy it is to keep vehicle-use records, in Chapter Nine the rules for keeping audit-proof business travel records, and in Chapter Ten the easy (but strict) rules regarding deductions for Meals and Entertainment expenses.

The National Taxpayers Union estimates that the average taxpayer spent 26.5 hours last year completing their tax returns.

In this Chapter you will learn THREE OPTIONS for documenting ALL of your day to day business income and expenses in **about a minute a day -- *literally*!**

OPTION 1: Even if you have only the smallest amount of computer savvy you can record the IRS-required records into an easy-to-use software program that will store, consolidate and tabulate all your deductions. **It takes only about a minute a day!**

At the end of the year, at the "press of a button," so to speak, your deductions are compiled and totaled, exactly the way the numbers are to be reported on your IRS Schedule C (Record of Profit and Loss from Business). Download a 30-day trial copy of the ***Home Business Tax Records Made Easy!*** software at **www.HomeBusinessTaxSavings.com.**

OPTION TWO: If you prefer an easy to use a 'manual' system for tracking and documenting your business income, expenses and activity, check out the ***Tax MiniMi$er***™, available at **www.HomeBusinessTaxSavings.com.** The 12 monthly spreadsheet-like forms have all the categories needed to "prompt" you to record all the data you will want for tax preparation at year-end. And each of the recordkeeping forms has a 'built-in' envelope, allowing you conveniently store your receipts chronologically for easy referral.

This is an amazingly easy (yet totally complete) 'pencil & paper' method of organizing all of your business records. "A dull pencil remembers better than the sharpest memory."

OPTION THREE: As a <u>bare minimum</u>, set up 9 file folders or 9 slots in an accordion file to store your receipts in the major Schedule C business expense categories.

Here are your file folder labels:

1. ADVERTISING and PROMOTION
(These expenses relate to line 8 of Schedule C)

2. VEHICLE OPERATING COSTS
(These expenses relate to lines 10 and 20 of Schedule C)

3. LEASE or PURCHASE of BUSINESS ASSETS
(These expenses relate to lines 13 and 20 of Schedule C)

4. WAGES, COMMISSIONS & EMPLOYEE BENEFITS PAID
(These expenses relate to lines 14, 19 and 26 of Schedule C)

5. LEGAL AND PROFESSIONAL FEES AND COSTS
(These expenses relate to line 17 of Schedule C)

6. BUSINESS USE OF YOUR HOME
(These expenses relate to line 30 of Schedule C and Form 8829)

7. OFFICE SUPPLIES
(These expenses relate to line 22 of Schedule C)

8. BUSINESS TRAVEL AND ENTERTAINMENT
(These expenses relate to line 24 of Schedule C)

9. MISC. OTHER BUSINESS EXPENSES

A Very Important Note About Recordkeeping

Most people <u>do</u> know that they need to keep copies of invoices or bills to document their tax-deductible expenses.

But many people do <u>not</u> know that they <u>also</u> are required to be able to prove they <u>paid</u> those invoices/bills. Proof of payment IS a requirement for making those expenses deductible.

The logic is not difficult to understand:

A taxpayer could order a $5,000 piece of business equipment, receive an invoice for it, but then cancel the order. If the IRS required only the invoice for documentation, the taxpayer could claim a $5,000 deduction for a piece of equipment he/she never received or paid for.

Therefore, the IRS requires the taxpayer to provide proof of the **cost of the item** (invoice) **and** proof that it was **paid**.

First, that proof could be in the form of a "PAID" stamp on the invoice, if the item was paid for in cash. Second, it could be documented with a cancelled business check. (If your bank provides only <u>copies</u> of your checks, be sure you have a copy of <u>both sides</u> of the check!)

The third option may be the best. If you use a business-only charge card to purchase a tax-deductible item, the IRS considers the item to have been *paid for* in the ***month the transaction appears on your statement***, even if you actually pay for the item later or over a period of time.

Example: You purchase a $2,000 computer (for business-use-only) on March 20, and charge the full amount to your credit card. In April you receive your monthly statement for transactions you made in March, and it lists the $2,000 purchase. For tax purposes, the full $2,000 amount is treated <u>as if you had paid for it in full on March 20th</u>, even though you may take many months to pay it off.

Therefore, your proof-of-*purchase* and proof-of-*payment*, **both** will be considered fully documented simply by keeping a copy of the monthly statement listing the charge.

By the way,

For smaller amounts, usually up to $75 per individual expense, notations in your tax deduction recordkeeping system or in your daily appointment calendar is accepted as proof of purchase. Exceptions are costs of commercial transportation and lodging, both of which require actual receipts regardless of the amount.

**Take a free 30-day 'test drive' of
Home Business Tax Records Made Easy! software
at www.HomeBusinessTaxSavings.com**

Your Tax Preparer can only be a good as the records YOU keep, so remember: "A dull pencil remembers better than the sharpest memory." Timely record keeping is the key to maximum (and bullet-proof) deductions. Check out the Tax MiniMi$er for a simple, but complete, recordkeeping system.

CHAPTER TWELVE

Easy Steps to "Bullet-Proofing" Your Tax Returns

"Bullet-Proof," as we use the term in this book, means that if you **are** audited, you will have the IRS-compliant documentation to validate every deduction you claimed on your Tax Return.

BIG TIP: The #1 Reason for audits: Math errors on the Tax Return. No kidding! #2 Reason: Incorrect Social Security number on the tax form. Seriously, those are #1 and #2. You definitely do **not** want to _invite_ an audit, so double and triple check all of your calculations, and make sure your SSN is recorded correctly.

When most taxpayers hear the word "audit" they get the same "in the gut" feeling they get when they look in the rear-view mirror and see flashing blue lights behind them. And for good reason.

The IRS will feed the Treasury Department some **$2 TRILLION** this year. And that's <u>before</u> audits.

Audits will rake in an *additional* <u>$50-BILLION!</u>

So first, let's put "audit" into perspective. An audit is nothing more than an attempt to see if you reported all of your income accurately, and if you qualified for all of the deductions you claimed.

If you are driving 65 MPH in a 65 MPH zone, you have nothing to fear if a highway patrolman uses radar to check your speed, right? Well, likewise, if all of the deductions you are claiming on your Tax Returns are legal and adequately documented, there's no reason to fear an audit.

Maintaining the required documentation does **not** have to be tedious, does **not** require a high-priced CPA to keep your books, (although I do highly recommend a professional bookkeeper), and does **not** take a lot of time, as we have just discussed in the previous chapter.

These are the *5 Most Important Steps* every taxpayer should take to 'Bullet-Proof' their Tax Returns...

1. **When documenting deductions**, be sure that you can produce evidence that you incurred the expense, which is usually going to be a copy of your invoice or a notation in your scheduling calendar or daily diary. And *also* be sure that you can prove that you *paid* the invoice. So keep your cancelled checks attached to your invoices for all

expenses you are deducting on your Tax Return. (Remember, when an expense is charged to a credit card, it is deemed to have been paid when the card charge is incurred, so keep credit card statements also.)

2. Many people who have an active home-based business, **keep a separate checking account for their business** income and business expenses, which is *highly* recommended. But you must know this: **ALL deposits into that account will be considered "earned income"** (i.e., taxable!) unless your checkbook register is annotated to indicate otherwise. If they add up your deposits and come up with a different number than you reported as gross income, it may look like you under-reported your income. (That's not a good thing!) Perhaps some of your deposits were personal funds you were loaning your company so that you could buy promotional materials. Solution: Mark clearly in your checkbook register the source (and sometimes, purpose) of every deposit into your business account.

3. **If you hire your children and/or spouse** in order to deduct their wages, you should…

> (a) Have (or get) an EIN Employer Identification Number.
>
> (b) Use a Family Member Employment Agreement, to specify the duties they will perform, the amount you will pay them, etc.
>
> (c) Document the work they performed. For example, they could turn in monthly or weekly calendar pages or timesheets on which they've recorded the work they did and what days they did it on.

(d) Pay them on a regular and consistent basis, and always pay them with a Business Check.

(e) Withhold, and pay, Social Security and Medicare taxes on adult family member employees (18 years and older).

You may also be required to show that the amount you are paying your family members is **"reasonable."**

One way you could do that would be to get an outside company to give you a written estimate for doing the same work, and then pay your family member approximately that amount or a little less. Or determine what a "reasonable person" might pay an employee or outside contractor for a similar service, and then use a comparable wage or salary.

4. If your Schedule C shows your home-based business **with a net loss for the year**, an auditor may require you to prove that you are working toward making a profit. Profit-intent is required, in order to prove that you are in a legitimate business. A Business Plan can be an important part of your proof. **So have a Business Plan.** Be sure to also follow the other recommendations in Chapter Two.

> **You can download a FREE fill-in-the-blanks Business Plan in the www.HomeBusinessTaxSavings.com**

5. **Never attend a tax-audit in person** (see next section). Retain a tax professional, such as an Enrolled Agent, CPA or Tax Attorney, and give them a Limited Power of Attorney to attend the audit in your place.

WHY & WHEN You Should NEVER Attend Your Own Tax Audit!

You **never** want to show up **in person** – or at least not alone – for a tax audit! **Never, never, NEVER!** Always have an Enrolled Agent, CPA or other IRS-approved representative **who has lots of *successful* audit experience** appear in your place.

If you try to go it alone, here's what you can expect.

- First, you'll be walking into an adversarial climate, where you know (or they'll remind you) that you are probably have missing or incomplete records. A bully attitude and heavy-handed tactics used frequently by some auditors will intimidate almost any taxpayer.

- They'll fire question-after-question at you, while implying that you should have immediate answers. If you take a minute to think about a question (after all, they're questioning details on a tax return you filed two or three years ago!), they'll give you "the look." You know -- the one that says, "I know you're guilty, so don't try to weasel your way out of it."

- They'll *lead you* like a good lawyer, into saying things that will cost you some of your tax deductions.

- No one has perfect records, but some IRS Auditors can make you feel like yours are among the worst ever.

Whether they admit it or not, the career progression of an auditor IS related to the number of "successful" audits he/she completes. Take a guess what "successful" means. You're right!

Audits brought in an extra **$50-<u>B</u>ILLION** to the U.S. Treasury last year. Most of that came *not* from people who were trying to cheat. It came from honest taxpayers who didn't keep all their receipts or records, or who "spoke before thinking" while in the pressure cooker of an audit.

Why would you put yourself through that if there is another way?

If you have an Enrolled Agent, for example, attend your audit <u>without you</u>, the auditor can't put you on the spot and expect you to spontaneously provide an answer to every little question. If you are **not** personally present, you cannot answer questions about "apparent discrepancies" – questions that may cause you to answer inaccurately, simply due to vague recollections of something that occurred up to three years ago.

If the auditor asks your <u>representative</u> a question he/she does not have the answer to, he'll just say, "I don't have the answer to that, but I'll be glad to get with my client (you) and get back to you with the answer."

That buys you time to think about the answer, or to check your records for an explanation. I do <u>not</u> mean time to "make up a lie." I mean time to <u>remember the truth</u> -- without a heavy handed auditor breathing down your neck.

Even if you think you have all the answers, there is another *big* reason to have a tax professional represent you. The whole climate changes when an auditor is meeting alone with a "fellow professional," as opposed to meeting with a "lying, cheating taxpayer." A really good tax pro who is experienced in audit representation, will quickly get the auditor feeling that your representative is there "to help determine the accuracy of the tax return in question." That gets the Auditor a bit more relaxed, feeling that "we're *both* on the side of truth, justice and the American way" – or close, at least.

Have no doubt, however, your tax professional is representing **YOU** and YOUR interest *only*. It's just that the more he or she can put the auditor at ease, the better the outcome will likely be for you.

"Nothing to Fear, But Fear Itself"

If you use one of the three systems reviewed in Chapter Eleven to keep good records, and use those records to have your taxes prepared by a home-business tax-law specialist, **you will have nothing to fear, even if you receive an audit notice**.

If all the deductions you claimed are legal, and if you've kept necessary records (both of which are described in this book), an audit of your Tax

Return will simply be an "unavoidable inconvenience." But it will not be something to be feared!

An Audit Can Actually be a Good Thing ---- Really!

On average, your chances of being randomly audited are just over 1%. That's about one chance out of every 100 taxpayers.

But if YOU *are* audited, *your* chances are 1 out of 1 – 100%. But you've followed the rules and have the required records, there's nothing for an auditor to "find." So, here's the good news about having a "random audit"…

If the result of your audit is "No Change," your chances of being audited again have significantly decreased. In fact the law protects taxpayers from multiple audits over similar issues when prior audits have confirmed the accuracy of the prior returns.

So, audits are rare, but they do happen. But "if you're driving within the speed limit, there's no reason to fear radar."

What "Triggers" an Audit?

The majority are "random audits," which means the computer picked you at random. If this happens, you will receive a love note in the mail suggesting that you two get together for a chat – otherwise known as an "Audit Notice." Don't take it personally. Blame the computer.

Many others are "Correspondence Audits," meaning they are handled through the mail. Others are done in person. They'll look over your entire return, not focusing on any one thing, unless they see something worth probing. See the previous section, labeled "Why & When You Should NEVER Attend Your Own Tax Audit!" That recommendation applies also to Random Audits.

Sometimes that same ugly computer is kicking out Tax Returns because something attracted its attention. The best way to attract its attention is to fail to report all of your 1099 and W-2 income. The IRS gets an attitude when a taxpayer has <u>un</u>reported or <u>under</u>reported income, and they'll send you one of those love notes.

In case you didn't know, one of the biggest "improvements" to the IRS' computer capability, is a sophisticated ability to match 1099s and W-2s to the individual taxpayer's Tax Return. If they have a 1099 on file which didn't show up on the taxpayer's return, the computer generates an "Oops" message, and sends it to the Audit division.

Sometimes that nasty computer kicks out a Tax Return because the taxpayer claimed a deduction amount that was "outside the normal range" for your particular business type. (That's why the signature line on the 1040 Tax Return form asks you to identify your occupation– which you are NOT required to provide, by the way.) That does NOT automatically generate an audit. It does automatically generate a review by a real person or an IRS middle-manager, who will determine whether or not auditing that specific return is likely to net the Treasury any additional money.

What's a "Disclosure Statement?" Your Most POWERFUL Protection in an Audit!

If you know that you are claiming a deduction that is likely to be outside the normal range for most people in your industry, here's something worth considering… Instead of waiting to give your explanation to an auditor, you can actually explain <u>in advance</u>. There is a little-known IRS Form number 8275, called a "Disclosure Statement" which you can attach to your Tax Return (obviously, you can't file electronically if you want to attach an 8275).

A "Disclosure Statement" could be called a "Let Me Explain" note, because that is what you would use it for. Since Tax Returns are processed by computers, you are not drawing attention to yourself by attaching a Form 8275. No human being (nor IRS employee) will see your 8275 unless the computer raises its hand and says "Hey, look at this one."

When that Return is reviewed, the reviewer sees your Disclosure Statement. If you have explained the situation adequately, your Return will likely be put back in the file drawer and you will have avoided an audit.

To add even more power to your Disclosure Statement, you could type these words at the bottom of the form:

> *"Under Penalty of Perjury, I swear that the above is*
> *true, accurate and complete, to the best of my knowledge"*

and then have your signature on that form **Notarized**.

The words "under penalty of perjury," means "If you can prove that I am lying, I know you could send me to jail." Do you think your Disclosure Statement might be even *more* believable with that Notarized statement at the end? If you're telling the truth, there's no risk in adding that statement.

The **most powerful, least understood** and **most under-used** of all IRS Forms is **Form 8275 – "Disclosure Statement."** This is how you **prove the un-provable.**

I call this the form that *"Tells them the answer, so they don't ask you the question."* In the "old days" a person could say "my word is my bond," or "my handshake is my commitment." Not anymore, and *especially* not with the IRS. How do you prove that your home-office is used exclusively for business? How do you prove that your kids actually *performed* the work you *hired* (and *paid*) them to do? How do you prove that "reconstructed records" are accurate? Use Form 8275.

Form 8275 is SO IMPORTANT – and so lacking in awareness – that we have written a Special Report on the incredible value of this form and how to use it, and it is available to you as a FREE download in the Resource Center www.HomeBusinessTaxSavings.com

---

Audits Aren't the Only Way
They Get their Hands on Your Wallet

Have you ever received a letter from the IRS stating that their records indicate that _two years ago_ you earned interest on your savings account but failed to report that income on your tax return. The amount they ask for is often way more than you would have owed initially, because by waiting for two years to bill you, they were able to tack on interest and penalties. The letter ends by saying "if you agree, then just send us the money."

Most people just mail in a check for the amount requested, _without even checking their own records to see if the IRS is right_. But many of those computer generated letters are flat out wrong!

Even worse is a widespread practice of sending out "Correction Notices." The IRS sends out a gazillion letters (that are not even written very well) printed in plain black ink on cheap white paper – and mail them _postage-free_! – asking for a specific amount of money. Why? The notice claims "we have recalculated your taxes and have found that you own an additional $347.96 (or whatever). The letter makes NO MENTION of what calculations resulted in that new number. And, to throw you into a panic, the letter tells you that the full amount needs to be paid by a date that often is less than two weeks away "in order to avoid additional interest and penalties."

Sounds scary, doesn't it? So most people who get those letters _immediately_ write a check for the full amount asked for, and mail it in on the very same day. Those letters collect over $2 Billion in cash --- yet **they are *wrong* about 80% of the time.** But they keep running their money-making campaign *successfully* year after year after year, for one reason – it works!!

Undoubtedly this will go down in history as the most successful and lowest cost (even though unscrupulous) fundraising campaign of all time!

DON'T FALL FOR IT. DO THIS INSTEAD...

The key to challenging correction notices is remarkably simple. You must write a letter declaring that you disagree with the IRS's "opinion" that you owe additional money. The authority for your response is Internal Revenue Code Section 6213(b)(2), which reads, "a taxpayer may file with the Secretary within 60 days after notice is sent under paragraph (1) a request for an abatement of any assessment specified in such notice, and upon receipt of such request, the Secretary shall abate the assessment."

What is **abatement**?" Abatement is the process of canceling the debt as though it never existed.

Very few tax laws are simpler than this. You have sixty days from the date of the notice to respond by "filing a request for abatement." If you do, <u>the IRS has no choice but to</u> "<u>abate the assessment</u>."

Please note that the law affords the IRS no latitude in complying with your request. The IRS may not dispute or ignore your timely written request. What's more, you have no burden of proof on the issue. The statute does not say you must "prove the notice is wrong" in order to win the abatement. It merely states that the IRS "shall abate the assessment" upon demand.

> The above is excerpted from Daniel J. Pilla's book, **"The IRS Problem Solver,"** named the #1 Tax Help Book by the *Wall Street Journal*. This book is a must have for every taxpayer, and is available in the Products & Services section of www.HomeBusinessTaxSavings.com

You do NOT Need to File by April 15th

You may know that if you file an IRS Form 4868 prior to April 15, you can get an *automatic* SIX month extension on your tax filing deadline. That slides your deadline to October 15 **-- six months after** the vast majority of taxpayers have filed.

Note: Prior to January 2006, taxpayers were required to file for an automatic FOUR month extension, and <u>then</u> *apply for* an additional TWO month extension. **Now** they are combined into **one six-month extension**, and its approval is automatic.

Some people hold off until October 15 to file <u>every year</u>. Their theory is that it substantially cuts their chances of getting 'selected' for a Random Audit. Why? Well, if the IRS computer is programmed to select a million returns for Random Audits, it's going to start selecting those names immediately on (or even before) April 15.

The thinking of these "late filers" is that, by October 15, the computer will have already reached its pre-determined limit for Random Audits. If that's true, then their chance of being selected for a Random Audit would drop from about 1 percent, to *zero percent*.

I can't confirm that their rationale is correct, but it certainly is an interesting theory, isn't it?

IMPORTANT:

An "Extension of Time to File" is **NOT** an Extension of time to **PAY**.

April 15th is *always* the deadline for paying **ALL** taxes due.

To save you the time of fishing around the IRS web site for the forms you need, you can download the ones most frequently used by small business owners, by clicking on the tab labeled "IRS Docs, Forms & Publications" at www.HomeBusinessTaxSavings.com

CHAPTER THIRTEEN

When Your Tax *Deductions* <u>Go Up</u>, the Tax You'll *Pay* will <u>Go Down</u>. So… Your Paycheck gets Bigger!

Do you remember your first day on the job, when you had to fill out all sorts of paperwork? One of those papers was a W-4 Tax Withholding Form, on which you wrote the number of **Allowances** to claim.

That number, coupled with your answer to whether your filing status was Single or Married, told your employer what percentage of your money he or she is required to withhold from your wages for various Federal and State taxes.

FIRST, a Misconception Many People have about W-4s…

The term "**Allowances**" has <u>nothing</u> to do with the number of people in your family or household.

The term *Allowances* does **<u>not</u>** mean "*Dependents*."

The term *Allowances* does **<u>not</u>** mean "*Exemptions*."

"Allowances" is simply a number that gets plugged into a formula to determine the amount of your wages to be withheld for taxes.

For example, if you claim <u>two</u> Allowances, a certain amount of your wages will be withheld for taxes. If you later file a revised W-4, lowering your Allowances to <u>one</u>, much <u>more</u> will be withheld from your paycheck, which will <u>decrease</u> your <u>take-home pay</u>. Or, if you change your W-4 to increase the number from two to <u>three</u>, then <u>less</u> money will be withheld from each paycheck for taxes, which will <u>increase</u> your take-home pay.

Most people do not understand the purpose of withholding taxes. If you've ever owned a home, you probably understand the term "escrow." It means that, with each month's house payment, the mortgage company is collecting (in <u>addition</u> to principal and interest), 1/12th of your annual Property Taxes.

That way, when the tax bill arrives, your mortgage company has the money to pay it for you. Assuming your property tax amount does not change midyear, when the bill comes in the mortgage company will have "in your escrow account," exactly the amount needed to pay it off.

Withholding taxes work exactly the same way. The number of Allowances you put on your W-4, is related to how much you expect to owe in Income Taxes during the course of the year. The employer, then, deducts a pro rata amount from each paycheck.

To use round numbers, let's say you expect to pay $12,000 in Income Taxes this year. If you get paid once a month, you want your employer to withhold $1,000 from each of your 12 monthly paychecks. If you get paid twice a month, you want your employer to withhold $500 out of each of your 24 paychecks.

In each case, the amount withheld during the course of the entire year, should come out to exactly what you owe in taxes. If the number of your Allowances was computed accurately, at the end of the year you will owe no additional taxes, and you will get no tax refund.

That's the way it <u>should</u> be.

If your withholding wasn't enough (because you claimed too many Allowances), you'll end up owing the government additional taxes at the end of the year. If you've had too much withheld (because you claimed <u>too few</u> Allowances), you'll end up getting a refund at the end of the year.

Contrary to popular opinion, **a Refund is NOT a good thing**! Getting a refund does not mean the IRS got religion in April. It means that you have been giving Uncle Sam a loan -- interest-free -- for a full year. Most people would be excited to get a $2,400 Tax Refund, however, what that <u>really</u> means is that, an extra $200 cash that <u>could</u> have been in <u>your own pocket</u> every single month, instead went to the government as an interest-free loan.

Many people believe that if they claim a high number of Allowances on their W-4 they're more likely to get audited. That just is not true, as long as the number of allowances is appropriate for your circumstances. Some people believe that if you claim more than a certain number, your employer has to notify the IRS. That requirement ended years ago.

If you *were* claiming <u>**4**</u> Allowances, and then changed your W-4 to claim <u>**8**</u> Allowances, and then, at the end of the year, you ended up owing $3,000 in additional Income Taxes… well, let's just say **that's <u>not</u> a good thing**. It's called "under-withholding." The objective is to make the amount of money withheld from your paycheck come out to almost exactly what your annual tax obligation will be.

If Your <u>Tax *DEDUCTIONS*</u> are <u>INcreasing</u>

(thanks to running your home-based business)

Your Tax <u>*WITHHOLDING*</u> should be <u>DEcreasing</u>

Nationwide, the average amount of taxes on income (including Federal and State taxes, Social Security and Medicare taxes) approaches 40% (or more!), meaning about $4 out of every $10 you earn gets gobbled up for various taxes, and then you get to live on the leftovers, called your "take-home pay."

> **This is VERY Important!** You are about to learn how you could increase your take-home pay, easily, legally and quickly -- IF you have a qualifying home-based business or have been receiving large year-end tax refunds (indicating over-payment of taxes). Never file a revised W-4 without first consulting with your tax professional.

To repeat what we said earlier, the amount of money withheld during the course of the year <u>should match</u> your tax obligation for the full year. If this happens, you owe no additional taxes and you get no refund at the end of the year.

But if too *little* was withheld, you'll end up having to send in a check with your Tax Return. And if too *much* was withheld, you'll get a Refund, which we've explained is not a good thing!

If you already have a home-business that will allow you to qualify for the deductions described in this book, and if knowledge of these deductions is **<u>new</u> to you**, you will probably begin owing a **lot *less* in taxes** than you have been paying.

When less money will be withheld from each paycheck for taxes, it means a larger check on payday! **<u>Every</u> payday!**

Anyone may submit a revised W-4 any time that your tax circumstances have changed. Once you have completed the following W-4 Allowance Estimator or your tax advisor has computed how much you will be saving in taxes due to the home-business tax breaks you've just learned about, you simply go to your payroll office and fill out a new W-4, claiming the number of allowances you and your tax advisor have determined to be appropriate. Be conservative, but also be realistic.

VERY IMPORTANT ADVICE:

If you want to get an idea of how many additional Allowances you could add to your W-4, you will find a"W-4 Allowance Estimator" in the next Chapter.

You are advised to reassess your withholding requirements every 90 days, and to make adjustments to your W-4 as necessary to account for changes in business income or business expenses. That's because your W-4 allowances are always based on your best estimates of future income and expenses. But, from time to time, you may find that your income is increasing faster or slower than you had estimated, or that your expenses are turning out to be higher or lower than earlier estimates. No problem, just keep making 'mid-course adjustments' as-needed by revising your number of allowances.

ALWAYS consult with a professional tax preparer who is experienced in home-business tax law before changing your W-4. If you need a free referral, check out "Professionals we Recommend" in the Resource Center at www.HomeBusinessTaxSavings.com

---

CHAPTER FOURTEEN

Putting It All Together

What have we learned, and what does it mean **to YOU?**

First, we have learned that America has two tax systems, and either you have been in the wrong one, or you have been in the right one, but lack of knowledge has kept you from getting all the tax-reduction benefits for which you could qualify.

Either way, you will no longer lose out on legitimate tax breaks just because no one ever told you about them, because now you know.

Before you read this book, if I had asked you, "Who in America gets the most tax breaks?" what would you have replied? Most people would have said, "The wealthy people who can afford good tax lawyers to find them all the loopholes."

But that really isn't true, is it? It's the people who establish and run a legitimate small or home-based business, *and* understand the tax laws that were enacted by Congress to encourage them to do just that. Those are the people who get the greatest number of legitimate tax breaks – people like YOU.

How Much Could YOU Save in Taxes?

Let's add up all the new tax-deductions you could qualify for:

- Flip back to Chapter Four. How many dollars worth of expenses did you calculate you'll be able to qualify as tax-deductible business expenses? (Remember, there are tax-deduction limits in the category called Indirect Expenses.) See last page of Chapter Four. **Record this number on line "A" on the following worksheet.**

- Will you hire your children as employees of your home-based business? If so, how many kids, and how much will you pay them? Remember, each child can earn up to $5,700 tax free in 2010. These wages are tax-deductible to you, and tax-free to them. **Put this number on line "B" on the following worksheet.**

- Will you be employing a spouse in your business, and giving him/her self-insured medical/dental benefits as discussed in Chapter Seven? This strategy lets you deduct all the out-of-pocket medical related expenses incurred by all members of your family. Expenses like annual deductibles, co-pays, non-covered medications, medical devices and procedures, over-the-counter drugs, etc. **Put that amount, plus employer-paid payroll taxes, on line "C" on the following worksheet.**

- Look back at Chapter Eight again. How much do you estimate you will be able to write-off for business use of your vehicle(s)? At a bare minimum, it will be the number of business miles times 50¢/mile (in 2010). Depending on your business vehicle use, this might come out somewhere between $3,500 and $5,000 – maybe more, maybe less. **Put that amount on line "D."**

- How much do you estimate you'll spend on business travel (including business trips that include some "personal days")? See Chapter Nine. **Record that number on line "E" on the following worksheet.**

- Will you entertain business associates? Will you qualify to write-off meal and entertainment expenses? **50% of that number goes on line "F."**

- Finally, add up all other business deductions that didn't fall into one of these six categories, and **record the total on line "G."**

Let's add them up…

YOUR *Estimated* Deductions
Due to Operating a Home-Business

A. Home-related Business expenses: $ _____
   (See Chapter Four for **limits on deducting** Indirect Expenses.)

B. Wages for hiring children: $ _____

C. Family's non-reimbursed medical costs: $ _____

D. Vehicle Business Miles x 50¢/mile: $ _____

E. Business Travel: $ _____

F. 50% of Business Meals/Entertainment: $ _____

G. Other Deductions: (business equipment, $ _____
   loss on sale of home/car, depreciation, etc.)

_____

Estimated Total Deductions: $ _____

Are you shocked at that number?   Most people are totally blown-away!

With all these new tax deductions, should you add more Allowances to your W-4 so that more money shows up in your paycheck?   Turn the page and let's see…

W-4 ALLOWANCE <u>ESTIMATOR</u>

(ALWAYS get advice of a tax pro before changing your W-4.)

If you have a traditional "W-2 job" and are paid wages from an employer, you have a Form W-4 on file in your employer's payroll office. The number of "Allowances" you wrote on this form (which you filled out on your first day of employment) tells your employer how much of your wages to withhold for taxes.

The Internal Revenue Code (IRC § 3402 and related regulations) authorizes any employee to revise his/her W-4 whenever his/her tax situation changes. The IRS does not limit the number of times a taxpayer may change his/her W-4, nor how frequently it may be changed. It does, however, **require your employer to process the revised W-4 AND to adjust the amount withheld from your wages for taxes,** *effective with the very next pay period*.

<u>**Increasing**</u> the number of Allowances results in a <u>**larger**</u> paycheck!
<u>**Decreasing**</u> the number of Allowances results in a <u>**smaller**</u> paycheck!

If you actively operate a small or home-based business (even on a part time basis) with the intent to produce a profit, you may qualify for many deductions for which other taxpayers may not be eligible. Since more Deductions means paying less in taxes, you may be eligible to increase your number of allowances, putting much more of your wages into your take-home pay.

This **W-4 Allowance Estimator** will take you through a process of determining the *approximate* number of Allowances you *could* claim on your own W-4. If this number is higher or lower than the number on your current W-4, you may wish to consider submitting a revised W-4.

It is *highly recommended* that you have a Tax Professional who *specializes* in Small-Business Tax Law, review your worksheet and your conclusions. Ask for his/her Professional Opinion *prior to submitting* a revised W-4. It is further recommended that you perform this calculation <u>every 90 days</u> and make W-4 revisions whenever necessary.

Now let's see if *YOUR* Small-Business/Home-Business Tax Deductions will affect the number of Allowances on *YOUR* Form W-4…

'*DIRECT* EXPENSE DEDUCTIONS'

A. Estimated total **Gross Business Income** for this year: ▶ $_____

B. 1. How many **DEPENDENT CHILDREN** age 7+ will you employ? _____ children

2. How much will you pay each child this year? _____/year
(In 2010, the first $5,700 is tax-free to them.)

3. **Multiply (B1) x (B2):** $_____

C. 1. How many **BUSINESS MILES** will you drive your vehicle(s)? ___ mi./year

2. **Multiply the above number x $0.50/mile:** $_____

D. Will you **EMPLOY YOUR SPOUSE?** YES / NO

If YES, how much does your family spend annually on **Health Costs** $_____
that are not reimbursed under any health insurance plan:

E. 1. What is your total of your **TELEPHONE COSTS** for the year? $_____

2. What is your monthly rate for **1-line Basic Service only**: $_____

3. Multiply "b1" x 12 = $_____

4. Subtract line "c" from line "a." Result = **Deductible Telephone Costs** $_____

F. What is estimate of all other annual **Business Operating Costs:** $_____

G. Estimate your total expenses for **Overnight Business Travel this year** $_____

(including travel costs for employees)

H. Add 'B' through 'G' and record the total here ▶ ▶ $_____

I. Subtract line 'H' from line 'A' and Record the RESULT: $_____

If RESULT shown on line 'I' is a "LOSS:"
(i.e., line A is smaller than line H)
Divide line 'I' by $3,650.
The result is *Number of Additional Allowances* to
Add to the number on your Current W-4.
== *OR* ==
If RESULT shown on line 'I' is a "PROFIT:"
(i.e., line A is larger than line H)
Divide line 'I' by $3,650.
Record that number here: _____ and
... PROCEED TO NEXT PAGE ...

If the calculation on the previous page resulted in a PROFIT on line 'I', you may ALSO claim INdirect Expense Deductions, but *ONLY up to the amount of your Profit*. However, if your Indirect Expense deduction total is greater than your profit total, you do not "lose" the remaining deductions -- you may 'carry forward' any remaining Indirect Expense Deductions for use on any *future* Tax Return.

Estimating Your
"INDIRECT EXPENSE" DEDUCTIONS

First, calculate the "BUSINESS-USE PERCENTAGE" of your home:

What is the total square-footage of the finished area of your home?

_____sq. ft.

What is the total square-footage of all areas of your home that you will use *"Regularly and Exclusively"* for business purposes?   _____sq. ft.

Bottom line divided by Top line = "Business-Use Percentage" (BUP).

Your BUP =_____%

J.   Estimate your annual total cost of ALL Utilities: $_____

Multiply the above number by your BUP % = $_____

K.   Annual Homeowner's or Renter's Insurance: $_____

Multiply the above number by your BUP % = $_____

L.   Annual estimated Repair & Maintenance costs: $_____

Multiply the above number by your BUP % = $_____

M.   If you **RENT**, your rent for the entire year = $_____

Multiply the above number by your BUP % = $_____

N.   TOTAL of lines 'A' through 'D' =   ►   ►   ►$_____

HOW TO *ESTIMATE* YOUR W-4 ALLOWANCE CHANGES:

Divide the *smaller* of line 'N' or line 'I' by $3,650, and add that number to the total you filled-in on the line at the very bottom of the previous page. The total of those two numbers represents the additional Allowances you could add to the number on your current W-4. **BUT CONSULT WITH A TAX PRO FIRST!**

CHAPTER FIFTEEN

You Could Get ANOTHER Even BIGGER Refund on Tax Returns You've Already Filed

Here is some good news! You have up to three years to file an Amended Tax Return (Form 1040X) any time you discover errors or oversights on a previous year's Tax Return! That includes deductions you missed out on!

Did you have a home-based business <u>prior</u> to this year? Are you kicking yourself because you could have paid a lot LESS in taxes if you had known <u>then</u> about the tax deductions you learned about just <u>now</u>?

Does it make you angry to think of all the extra money that you gave Uncle Sam, <u>just because you didn't know the things you've learned from this book?</u>

Don't get angry, get even!

Guess what? If the IRS ends up owing you an additional refund (as they probably will), **they'll also pay you interest** for the time they had your money!

How much could this be worth? Using old calendars and day planners and scheduling diaries will help you remember many of your deductible expenses, but not all of them, of course. Even if you can reconstruct only half of the deductions you could have qualified for back then, it could still result in a $2,000 to $3,000 refund -- **per year** -- for up to **three years**!

That could mean a windfall of $6,000 to $9,000 *plus interest!* Cool, huh! You get there by filing a Form 1040X "Amended Individual Tax Return" for any of the past three years in which you operated a legitimate home-based business.

When some people hear this amazing news, their reflex reaction is, "My tax returns aren't perfect; I don't want to give them a reason to look at them a second time." Or they blurt out, "I don't want to get audited."

That is proof-positive that what you *don't* know *can* hurt you.

What really happens when your 1040X arrives at the IRS Service Center? First of all, it will draw zero attention, because millions of Amended Returns are filed every year. Do they look again at the original tax return? Of course, but only to make sure you haven't already claimed the same tax deductions on your original return. That's it.

If you had a home-based business in the past three years, have your prior years' returns reviewed by a tax professional who is a seasoned expert in home-business tax law.

Put that little item at the <u>very top</u> of your To-Do list! It may just put thousands of dollars of extra cash in your pocket, *quickly*!

For a referral to a small-business tax specialist who will review all of your past 3 years Federal Tax Returns visit www.HomeBusinessTaxSavings.com

FINAL THOUGHTS FROM THE AUTHOR

Congratulations on reading this book from start to finish. YOU now know more about home-business tax deductions than most tax preparers in this country! With this knowledge you will be able to keep more of your hard earned money in your own pocket, where it belongs.

So the question now is, what are you going to do with the thousands and thousands of dollars it will save you? May I offer a couple thoughts?

First, about that money you're saving…

Think of it as "free money," so try not to be too selfish with it. How about taking at least 10% and doing some good for others? Tithe it for God's work, or donate it to an orphanage, or give it to a library – just don't keep it all for yourself. It's all God's money anyway. Please try to be a good steward of His money. The remaining 90% should be more than enough to pay the costs of operating your home-based business.

Second, about the information you just learned …

You now know that when you stop overpaying your taxes, an extra four or five hundred dollars per month can show up in your pocket. Eighty percent of all bankruptcies occur for lack of a few hundred dollars a month. Homes go into foreclosure for lack of a few hundred dollars a month.

These things are happening right now – <u>today</u> – to tens of thousands of others **-- probably including people you know**! Now that you understand the tremendous value of this easy-to-use information, please accept the challenge – maybe even the *obligation* – to help "spread the word" to the millions of others who need to know what you now know. (If you join our free Affiliate program, we'll thank you with cash for every sale you refer.)

Finally --

Don't stop learning! There are *far more ways* to reduce your taxes to the legal minimum. When you join my **"Tax Savings Secrets Club"** you will receive a 20-30 minute video each week for 26 consecutive weeks, each containing a *new* tax savings strategy that goes *beyond those covered in this book*. You will learn an impressive amount of information, but you'll learn it in bite sized pieces, easy to understand and easy to use. Check it out at http://homebusinesstaxsavings.com/shop/tax-savings-secrets-club

May God bless You <u>and</u> your Business!

Ron Mueller, author

ABOUT THE AUTHOR

Ronald R. (Ron) Mueller is a baby-boomer, born in Sioux City, Iowa, the son of a career postal worker and a career bookkeeper. He left the Midwest in 1965 to accept an appointment to the United States Naval Academy in Annapolis, MD, where he earned a Bachelor's Degree in Business Management and was Commissioned as an Ensign in the United States Navy.

After volunteering to serve his country for eight years on active duty as a Naval Officer, including a combat tour in Vietnam, Ron worked as an investigative reporter for the Atlanta Journal, and then entered the business world, focusing on the fields of advertising and marketing. His many business successes included heading the Washington, DC offices of Ketchum Communications, Earle Palmer Brown Advertising, and Burson-Marsteller Marketing, plus two years as vice president of marketing communications for McDonnell Douglas Corp.

While holding these demanding positions, he was also advancing his education, earning a Master's in Communication from the University of Oklahoma, a Masters in Business Administration from The American

University, and a Ph. D. in business economics from Sacramento Regent University.

Ever since he was a young boy working as a caddy for several successful businessmen at his hometown Country Club, he heard repeatedly that real success comes to those who are self employed. Now this was quite a contrast from what he had learned from his parents -- that the way to get more money is to take on a second job. Years later, in 1999, having grown weary of his corporate 14-hour workdays and exhausting 4-hour daily commutes, Ron fired his boss and hired himself.

While building a successful career out of making other people's businesses thrive, he had learned this: **It's how much you *keep*, that counts, not how much you make**. So Step One in starting his own business was to gain a thorough understanding of small-business tax savings.

Right away many well-meaning friends began offering Ron the 'free advice' that home-based business owners get huge tax benefits. But not one of those well-meaning friends was able to tell him what those tax benefits *are*, or how to *qualify* for them, or what *records* he would need to keep. So he began spending hours in bookstores, on the Internet, and even in the United States Library of Congress looking for information about those "small business tax advantages."

Since he could find no useful resources on this subject, Ron drew on his earlier experience as an investigative reporter, and launched into doing his own research. After several months, what he had discovered was exciting. First of all, yes, small businesses *can* qualify for most of the same tax breaks as big businesses. Second, there are several *additional* tax breaks *specifically* for home-businesses owners. Third, the potential *value* of those tax benefits is *huge*. And finally, many of the largest tax breaks were authorized by Congress *specifically* to encourage and reward the start-up and running a small business.

Dr. Mueller was <u>not</u> looking for 'tax-dodges' or 'loopholes' or 'gray-areas,' so he traced every individual small-business tax break all the way back to the precise Article in the U.S. Tax Code, or the specific Congressional Tax Law, or the exact Federal Tax Court Ruling that authorized it.

By now Ron's Midwestern work ethic and Christian values began "screaming" that he needed to find a way to make this information available and affordable to every one of the 25 million small-business owners who need it –especially since many were unaware of how *much* they needed it.

His response to that inner passion was to write a step-by-step guide that explained, in *plain English*, what tax breaks are available to small businesses, how to qualify for them, and how to spend only a minute or two a day keeping the necessary records.

That book has become a bestseller. The first four editions were published under the title, *"It's How Much You KEEP, That Counts! Not how much you*

Make." The FIFTH Edition of that same book, renamed **"Home Business Tax Savings *MADE EASY!"*** is the book which you are now finishing.

Today, Ron Mueller devotes fulltime to sharing this information with home-business owners through live presentations, tele-conferences, webinars, writings, coaching and mentoring. "Captain Mueller" lives aboard a 60 foot, four level yacht in San Diego, California, which he has appropriately named "Home Office."

FOR MORE INFORMATION

to enhance your

Tax Savings & Business Success

visit

www.HomeBusinessTaxSavings.com

where you will find…

- Valuable *Tax Reduction* Information

- Important *Business Success* Tools

- Regular *Tax Tips* You Can Bank On

- Alerts whenever *Tax Laws Change*

- Downloadable *Special Reports*

- Easy-Use Tax Deduction *Recordkeeping Systems*

- Useful *IRS Documents*, Forms and Publications

- *Referrals to Experts* I Personally Know & Trust

- Timesaving *Links and Resources*, and even a

- Generous *Referral Rewards* affiliate program.

Visit us at
www.HomeBusinessTaxSavings.com
…and come back often!

Please see reverse side for reordering this book ► ► ►

FOR ADDITIONAL COPIES

OF

Home Business Tax Savings *Made Easy!*

Order Online at
www.HomeBusinessTaxSavings.com

Or to Order by Phone,

CALL (toll-free) 1-888-9-TAX-CUT

**Orders are Normally Shipped within 72 Hours,
usually via USPS *Priority Mail***

WE ACCEPT:

▶ CREDIT CARDS,
▶ DEBIT CARDS,
▶ POSTAL MONEY ORDERS &
▶ PERSONAL or BUSINESS CHECKS

FOR MORE INFORMATION

to enhance your

Tax Savings & Business Success

visit

www.HomeBusinessTaxSavings.com

where you will find…

- Valuable *Tax Reduction* Information
- Important *Business Success* Tools
- Regular *Tax Tips* You Can Bank On
- Alerts whenever *Tax Laws Change*
- Downloadable *Special Reports*
- Easy-Use Tax Deduction *Recordkeeping Systems*
- Useful *IRS Documents*, Forms and Publications
- *Referrals to Experts* I Personally Know & Trust
- Timesaving *Links and Resources*, and even a
- Generous *Referral Rewards* affiliate program.

Visit us at
www.HomeBusinessTaxSavings.com
…and come back often!

Please see reverse side for reordering this book ► ► ►

FOR ADDITIONAL COPIES

OF

Home Business Tax Savings *Made Easy!*

Order Online at
www.HomeBusinessTaxSavings.com

Or to Order by Phone,

CALL (toll-free) 1-888-9-TAX-CUT

**Orders are Normally Shipped within 72 Hours,
usually via USPS *Priority Mail***

WE ACCEPT:

▶ CREDIT CARDS,
　　▶ DEBIT CARDS,
　　　　▶ POSTAL MONEY ORDERS &
　　　　　　▶ PERSONAL or BUSINESS CHECKS